OUR FRUIT OF CHRISTIANITY

PROSPERITY

A 31-DAY DEVOTIONAL

CURRY PUBLISHING

OUR FRUIT OF CHRISTIANITY

PROSPERITY

A 31-DAY DEVOTIONAL

Tamra Ingram – Curry

ISBN: 979-8-9907655-2-8

Design and Production: by Tamra Ingram-Curry / FlutterBy Press

Published by: Curry Publishing
An imprint of Curry Publishing
tamraingramcurry.com
P.O. Box 415
Valley Springs, AR 72682

PROSPERITY

Our Fruits of Christianity Devotional Series

BOOK 3 Our Fruit of Prosperity

PROSPERITY
INTRODUCTION

Our Fruit of Christianity: Prosperity is the third book
in the series of Our Fruit of Christianity. Prosperity
explores the Fruits we can experience and enjoy from
our lives as Christians, and what prosperity can look
like and be according to the Word of God.
Unfortunately, the concept of prosperity today is
given a harsh view, but true prosperity, Biblical
prosperity is for the whole Body of Christ, all
believers. As long as you believe in the balanced
theme of prosperity, you will flourish in that
prosperity. The goal of this Devotional Series is not
to place boundaries on a Christians life, but it is to
celebrate some of the natural spiritual gifts that come
as a result to orderliness and perseverance in a life
lived according to the Bible. This devotion does not
tell you *how* to live but gives examples of fruit or
visual or palatable, with their physical results that
many Christians do experience, not necessarily fruit
you *should be* experiencing as some type of rule. We all
grow differently off the branch, but our job isn't to
dictate what we grow, but to cling tight to the branch
and allow God to minister to each of us individually
and according to the call He has placed on our lives.
Many times, this growth will birth fruit for us to enjoy
and even share our fruit with the rest of the Body of
Christ. As a body has many parts, so does the Body of
Christ have many parts, or people, who produce
various given gifts, talents, and calls directly from the
Branch. Fruit is for recognition, use and spiritual
food.

Each topic is scripture heavy, taken from the New
King James Version Bible, unless specified in the text.

Topic may reflect you and your walk, or some of the topics may be things you understand God developing in your life. None of the fruit discussed is a must to produce unless God directs it through His branch connection to you.

This devotional series is also not referring to the Fruit of the Spirit, even though the fruit given through the direction of the Holy Spirit is intertwined in many of the fruits being discussed, they are not to be confused with the fruits of the Spirit named in Galatians 5:22-23.

There is a study journal provided separate for each book in the series. The journal is available for readers who would like extra study and challenge questions to extend each day's devotion. The journal can be used in different ways.

- First by reading the main devotion for the day, and the next day going to the journal to further study the one day's devotion before moving forward to the next.
- The second way is the journal can be implemented each day as the reader reads a new devotion, which would require a longer study period for each day's devotion.
- The third way is doing the devotion as a small group, where the devotions are read each day, the journal questions are filled out before group or as a part of going through the week's devotionals answering the questions during group time.

PROSPERITY

It is up to the reader of course if the journal is something they want, but the devotional books are set up to be used without the journals as independent studies. It might be good to have at least a spiral notebook to take notes of your own during your study time and listen for the Lord to address you personally.

Colossians 1: 9-14

For this reason we also, since the day we heard it, do not cease to pray for you, and to ask that you may be filled with the knowledge of His will in all wisdom and spiritual understanding; that you may walk worthy of the Lord, fully pleasing Him, being fruitful in every good work and increasing in the knowledge of God; strengthened with all might, according to His glorious power, for all patience and longsuffering with joy; giving thanks to the Father who has qualified us to be partakers of the inheritance of the saints in the light. He has delivered us from the power of darkness and conveyed us into the kingdom of the Son of His love, in whom we have redemption through His blood, the forgiveness of sins.

I pray this prayer for each person who endeavors to study this devotional series, for the reasons mentioned in the prayer. I pray you are blessed by the reading of this devotional, and you can grow in Christ through its simple understandings.

Thank you for your purchase.

Tamra Ingram-Curry

OUR FRUITS OF CHRISTIANITY

CHAPTER 1

Our Fruit of Prosperity

PROSPERITY

DAY 1

Provision From Service: Who Gets It?

Reading Reference

Hebrews 9:15
And for this reason, He is the mediator. of the new covenant, by means of death, for the redemption of the transgressions, under the first covenant, that those who are called may receive the promise of the eternal inheritance.

Revelations 21:7 He who overcomes shall inherit all things and "I will be his God, and he shall be My son."

1Peter 1:3-5 Blessed be the God and Father of our abundant mercy has begotten us again to a living hope through the resurrection of Jesus Christ from the dead. To an inheritance incorruptible, and undefiled and that does not fade away, reserved in Heaven for you, who are kept by the power of God through faith for salvation ready to be revealed in the last time.

The goal of a Christian is to serve God every day. Serving God is not only a prosperous duty, but also it promotes the Kingdom of God further. Servin gets our minds off all the worldish things which can distract, even if those things are good. Serving God keeps us eternally minded, and takes the focus off of ourselves, which can happen easily without thinking.

Serving whether in the church, or in our place of work, day to day sets us up for success in so many ways, not only in prosperity and provision. We each have an assignment to carry out in our service to God. Thank goodness we all aren't preachers or evangelists, but we are bank tellers, who pray for our customers when the opportunity comes. We are grocery store baggers who get to help people with showing a Godly kindness and can be the perfect thing needed after a difficult day at work. We are factory workers, ministering to our friends on lunch break through the conversations we refuse to be involved in, as much as the ones we choose to partake in. He has called all of us to service in His kingdom, and his provision for what we need on this earth is a part of our salvation, like eternal life and healing are a part of salvation.

It would be out of balance to serve God for the single reason of receiving His provisions only. However, when we trust God, by faith, and any trust we place in Him to provide our needs, turn us to thankfulness towards him, or it does for me. That thankfulness then leads to further service and a special faith in His call. He sets the example we can exemplify towards others throughout the Bible in the life led by Jesus on earth.

If God is faithful... so am I.

If God is forgiving... so am I.

If God is trustworthy... so am I.

Being thankful and portraying the characteristics of God through our service to the church you attend creates a natural, peaceful, not worked-up, real life provision, both supernaturally and naturally.

I also want to add, if you get burned out, as some have in serving God, maybe the problem isn't your service but your efforts in the flesh. It could be that it's the wrong area of service you have stepped into or felt obligated to take over. Burnout also comes from being the one in need of learning boundaries. Some offices need more boundaries than other offices of service, as you could be taking on too many things outside the realms of, and which don't have anything to do with the call or service specifically chosen by God for your life. These extras duties may be very good, very Christian in nature, and a needed activity. However, it is still not something you personally need to take on. By taking on the extra duties, you are also taking away from someone else's harvest of provision to do that very service.

Prayer.

Father, help us to see and exhibit You every day in the things that we provide for others and in the services, we do for You. I pray You are blessed by our service to you and Your church. I pray we don't ever allow the flesh to take the role ahead of what You've called us to do. Thank You for prospering us because of our service. Thank You for prospering us in our service to You. Help us today as we go out to remember that the service is for You, and I pray our service blesses You. In Jesus' name, Amen.

DAY 2

Who Doesn't Receive Provision?

Reading Reference

Ephesians 5:1-5 NKJV Therefore be imitators of God as dear children. And walk in love, as Christ also has loved us and given Himself for us, an offering and a sacrifice to God for a sweet-smelling aroma.

But fornication and all uncleanness or covetousness, let it not even be named among you, as is fitting for saints; neither filthiness, nor foolish talking, nor coarse jesting, which are not fitting, but rather giving of thanks. For this you know that no fornicator, unclean person, nor covetous man, who is an idolater, has any inheritance in the kingdom of Christ and God.

Ephesians 5:15 NKJV See then that you walk circumspectly, not as fools, but as wise, redeeming the time, because the days are evil.

1 Corinthians 6:9-11 NKJV Do you not know that the unrighteous will not inherit the Kingdom of God? Do not be deceived. Neither fornicators, nor idolaters, nor adulterers, nor homosexuals, nor sodomites, nor thieves, nor covetous, nor drunkards, nor revilers, nor extortioners, will inherit the Kingdom of God. And such were some of you. But you were washed, but you were [c]sanctified, but you were justified in the name of the Lord Jesus and by the Spirit of our God.

I Timothy 6:3-6 NKJV If anyone teaches otherwise and does not consent to wholesome words. Even the words of our Lord Jesus Christ, and to the doctrine which accords with godliness, He is proud, knowing nothing, but is obsessed with disputes and arguments over words, from which come envy. Strife. Reviling. Evil suspicions. Useless wranglings of men, of corrupt minds, and destitute of the truth, who suppose that godliness is a means of gain. Period from such withdrawal yourself.

Let's continue the conversation today of our fruit of provision but from the perspective of who the Bible states will not receive God's provision.

I don't want to impress on you some black and white blanket-thought on why a person doesn't receive the provisions from God. Let's just look at this topic as guidelines, or boundary points for what could be the reason as to why provision isn't fully manifesting in your life. I use this qualifier because God is God and simply, we don't know all the why's, except the one's found in His word.

Personally, I have seen folks whom I know operate in one of these "no-no's" and still God's provision is very active in their life. However, just imagine what a more glorious life they could experience if they were brave enough to overcome the one little hangup in their life they dearly hold on to. Selah.

16

Ephesians 5: 1-5 shows very clearly some of the issues hindering God's provision. Verse, one says, 'therefore be imitators of God as dear children.' I want to pause here and say, this verse is exactly how one will receive full provision and how we are to be as little children. As other areas of the Bible suggest. Continuing in Ephesians, it says, "little children imitate the behaviors and attitudes of their parents. God as our Father deserves this from us. Ephesians 5:2 says, "and walk in love. (Our only commandment as New Testament believers) as Christ also has loved us and gives himself for us, an offering and a sacrifice to God for sweet smelling aroma."

Here's where the warning begins, and mind you, He is speaking to the Christian in these next few verses. Ephesians 5: 3-5 says, but fornication and all uncleanness or covetousness-let it. Not even be named among you, as is fitting for Saints: neither filthiness, nor foolish talking, nor coarse jesting, which are not fitting, but rather giving of thanks. For this you know that no fornicator, or unclean person, or covetousness, man who is an idolater, has any inheritance in the Kingdom of Christ and God.

1st Corinthians 6: 9 - 11. Goes into greater details of what unrighteousness and fornication are, for those of us who need an understanding of it. Verse 9 says, do you not know? (Implies that we should know, as it should have been taught in churches and understood as you read the Bible) that the unrighteous will not inherit the Kingdom of God? Do not be deceived. (By unbalanced teaching, or teachers of a wide acceptance in grace) neither

fornicators, idolaters, nor adulterers, nor
homosexuals, nor sodomites. (Those who participate
in sodomy-- not the citizens of Sodom and
Gomorrah) nor thieves, nor covetous, nor drunkards,
or revilers, nor extortioners will inherit the Kingdom
of God. Verse 11 of that same chapter says "And
such were some of you. But you were washed, but
you were sanctified., but you were justified in the
name of the Lord Jesus and by the Spirit of our God.

Even though we are new creations in Christ,
our flesh is still calling us to act like the old man
which was buried through salvation in Jesus. The
things mentioned must be laid down in the life of
every Christian to inherit the Kingdom of God. There
are no exceptions, there isn't a way around it. This is
one of the places the Bible is direct in the behaviors
of new believers. It is not acceptable to dabble in
fornication or a drunken lifestyle, but it is through the
powerful blood of Jesus that we will overcome those
hindrances to our future life on earth. These sins
listed are mentioned to every believer, regarding
deliberately walking away from any of those lifestyles,
so also don't start them. These are things we leave at
the cross, as they have no bearing on our new life in
Christ Jesus. These are some of the things Jesus died
on the cross and bore those sins in His body for our
full redemption. Because of that sacrifice our
redemption from them can be full, as long as we yield
them to the cross.

1 Timothy 6:3- 6 teaches "if anyone teaches
otherwise, and does not consent to wholesome
words, even the words of our Lord Jesus Christ and
to the doctrine which accords with godliness, he is

proud, knowing nothing, but is obsessed with disputes and arguments over words, from which come envy, strife, reviling, evil suspicions, useless wranglings of men of corrupt minds and destitute of truth, who suppose that godliness is a means of gain. From such withdraw yourself. Now godliness with contentment is great gain."

PRAYER

Father, we see in your word today the clear boundaries for receiving Your provisions. I ask that You work with us, along with Holy Spirit to work in us keeping us from crossing those boundaries knowingly. Father, I ask for help in repenting of anything we are unaware of that we are dabbling in which has been mentioned in the scriptures above as well. Lord, convict our hearts in these behaviors if we still hold to any one of them, and release them fully and finally forever. I pray for this so we can all walk in and fully partake of everything good you want to provide to us in our life here on earth. I ask this for each one studying this lesson today. In the name of Jesus, Amen.

PROSPERITY

Day 3

Provision By Simply Asking

Reading Reference

Psalm 2:8 NKJV Ask of Me, and I will give you the nations for Your inheritance, and the ends of the earth for Your possession.

Matthew 7: 7-8 NKJV Jesus said,
"Ask, and it will be given to you; seek, and you will find; knock, and it will be opened to you. For everyone who asks receives, and he who seeks finds, and to him who knocks it will be opened."

Luke 11: 9-10 NKJV "So I say to you, ask, and it will be given to you; seek, and you will find; knock, and it will be opened to you. For everyone who asks receives, and he who seeks finds, and to him who knocks it will be opened.

Matthew 7 and Luke 11, referenced above is when Jesus is teaching how to access provision in the Kingdom of God. Jesus is our portion, our supply and if He has all nations and has the ends of the earth as His – I AM provided for all. As I am in Him and He is in me, I simply need to ask for this provision.

One day I was laying my heart out before the Lord in conversation, and He stopped me abruptly. Obviously, I was getting pathetic in my desperate winy plea to Him. He said to my heart, "you have not, because you ask not."

I began to learn that day how simply asking God, as my child would ask me, for a new toy or permission to go to a friend's birthday party, really pleases His heart. A child always asks in faith, knowing they deserve a good answer from the parent.

I thought I has asked God for the situations I was at this point pleading about. When you plead to God, it's a good marker you have stepped out of faith as pleading with God in prayer is not, asking in faith. I noticed this after His simple statement and began to think back to the time I had asked. Without fail I had either not actually asked a direct question, or I had only mentioned the difficulties I was having without also asking for guidance, help or delivery.

Why had I not just asked? That answer can lie in a thousand pieces before me, and they matter little. The main issue was I never honestly brought it before Him and asked. Could it have been a pride issue that was disguised as honesty? Pride is a way to 'cop out' of asking by using an emotional plea, instead of just humbly asking for our very need.

PRAYER

Father, today as we go about our day remind us to seek You, to ask for the things that are hard to be resolved. Remind us how much we love our own children and help us notice how they approach us in asking for provision in their lives. May we learn to step back and be childlike with you, dependent and hopeful. I ask that we seek you and knock on the door of Your goodness every day. I ask this expecting with wide eyes the best answer from our Father. In the name of Jesus, amen.

PROSPERITY

Day 4

Historic Temple Provisions

Reading Reference

1 Chronicles 29:16 NKJV O Lord our God, all this abundance that we have prepared to build You ad house for Your holy name is from Your hand and is all Your own.

1 Kings 4: 27, 29 (7-34 in context) NKJV

And Solomon had twelve governors over all Israel, who provided for the king and his household; each one made provision for one month of the year.

27- And these governors, each man in his month, provided food for King Solomon and for all who came to King Solomon's table. There was no lack in their supply.

29 – And God gave Solomon wisdom and exceeding great understanding, and largeness of heart like the sand on the seashore.

The description of Solomons provision is key for us today as well. God blessed him greatly, but not only with possessions but wisdom, and favor among many nations also. But why?

Because Solomon honored God, honored His temple, His name was layered in Solomons wise words of the

PROSPERITY

Bible. It is in the chapters Solomon wrote we today can read the beautiful descriptions and wisdom of God's character and His heart through Solomon's voice of honor. A human doesn't usually write such words as Solomon has without being truly intimate and abiding alongside God himself.

Solomon's words are one of relationship and understanding, one of pureness of heart. It is obvious there he has a knowing of the Great I AM.

God made vast and various provisions for Solomon because Solomon's heart searched out God first.

Matthew 7:7-8

"Ask, and it will be given to you; seek, and you will find; knock, and it will be opened to you. For everyone who asks receives, and he who seeks finds, and to him who knocks it will be opened."

Luke 11:13 "if you then, being evil, know how to give good gifts to your children, how much more will your heavenly Father give the Holy Spirit to those who ask Him!"

Seek God first. Communicate with Him daily to find His desires for your life. He then has grounds to prosper you.

PRAYER

Father, may we turn our hearts and focus to You today and every day. As we seek You, dine with us at the table of provision. Keep our hearts balanced and focused on the forwarding of your kingdoms work with the many provisions You give. Make in us modern day Solomon's. Thank you, Father, we are grateful for the historical accounts showing us who You are and how you enjoy prospering us. Bless forever, the God who sees ahead! Amen.

PROSPERITY

Day 5

Today's Temple Provisions

Reading Reference

1 Corinthians 3: 16-17 NKJV Do you not know that you are the temple of God and that the Spirit of God dwells in you? If anyone defiles the temple of God, God will destroy him. For the temple of God is holy, which temple you are.

While the Jewish people wait to have the temple rebuilt, we the Body of Christ, The Church, are the temple of God in our redeemed position. Today's temple for us then is each person our own body. We are not to worship our bodies, but to worship Him who inhabits our bodies, or Jesus and Holy Spirit. We don't go to church buildings and pray to or worship the walls or curtains, windows or pews, nor the décor like pictures or statues or structures at church. No! That would be considered idol worship. We go inside the church building to join with others in the Spirit of God and to praise God, pray to God and worship God with our tithes, talents and service to His body of believers.

I think what is more important than doing the church scene, is to daily get quiet and meet personally with Holy Spirit, to worship in song and thankfulness to Jesus. The Holy Spirit lives in my spirit man, and He instructs and guides the decisions Christians make for life, but He also helps us to pound out the issues they may be facing which are challenging or traumatic.

In Romans 8 verse 6, they speak of the fruit coming from our temple, or body, as being life and peace. We might be living, or alive, but it is the Spirit Who brings prosperity and healing into our bodies, like that life and peace mentioned in Romans 8. Life and peace are more valuable than simple money or possessions. Don't get hung up when you hear pastors teach prosperity. Money or goods are only a small portion of the big index of prosperity being taught.

Romans 8:6 NKJV For to be carnally minded is death, but to be spiritually minded is life and peace.

Romans 8: 1, 11, 13 NKJV

1-There is therefore now no condemnation to those who are in Christ Jesus, who do not walk according to the flesh, but according to the Spirit.

11- But if the Spirit of Him who raised Jesus from the dead dwells in you, He who raised Christ from the dead will also give life to your mortal bodies through His Spirit who dwells in you.

13- For if you live according to the flesh you will die; but if by the Spirit you put to death the deeds of the body, you will live.

Prosperity includes peace. In fact, peace is the most prosperous thing God has provided to us. If you claim the prosperity gospel is not godly you are claiming peace is not godly and we should not have it. I think we could all use more peace in our daily walk. Prosperity also includes health and healing. If you claim the prosperity gospel is not a godly teaching, and you're against it, then you are claiming you are against owning a home, or car. You are against having a job that gives you a way to pay your electricity or mortgage every month. If you claim prosperity is wrong, I highly recommend you quitting your job, because you're going against your own claims against prosperity. You might sell your house and get to the place in your life where you have nothing to prosper from and live as a nomad in the streets, depending on literally no one for survival.

An example of prosperity in health and healing are the gardens we plant for food and seeking God that they produced high yields of food for our table. Prosperity is also praying and believing if we are business minded people, or landlords who rent houses for others to live in, that we will have paying considerate customers that are faithful in their support of our product. It's only when prosperity comes to being a part of the church concept or it is involving the pastor of that church that prosperity is considered wrong, but not for you or your own life. Am I right? I say there are a lot of things wrong with people who get so angry at the prosperity message. In reality, it's because they don't understand it fully, or maybe their understanding has been diluted by wrong education of the full gospel.

PROSPERITY

Prosperity is a vast concept, so don't knock the preacher who has a mandate to focus on teaching the topic. If you see money as the main way to be rich, just forgive yourself and open your heart to understanding what the Bible itself really says about us being prosperous and the various aspects of what it means to be prosperous.

Our temples house a wealth of prosperity through the working of the Holy Spirit. Allow Him to heal that misguided teaching that is so against the prosperity gospel.

PRAYER

Father, thank You for the Holy Spirit. Thank you for the many prosperous provisions You supply in our lives daily. Teach us to honor this temple which houses the Holy Spirit. Teach us to know and understand the importance of our temples. I ask this in the name of Jesus. Amen.

Day 6

God's Provision

Reading Reference

Proverbs 8:21 That I may cause those who love me to inherit wealth, that I may fill their treasuries.

Psalms 37:18-19 The Lord knows the days of the upright, and their inheritance shall be forever. They shall not be ashamed in the evil time, and in the days of famine they shall be satisfied.

Psalms 132:13-18 For the Lord has chosen Zion; He has desired it for His dwelling place: "This is My resting place forever; here I will dwell, for I have desired it. I will abundantly bless her provision; I will satisfy her poor with bread. I will also clothe her priests with salvation, and her saints shall shout aloud for joy. There I will make the horn of David grow; I will prepare a lamp for My Anointed. His enemies I will clothe with shame, but upon Himself His crown shall flourish."

We may go to work every day outside our homes, yet some may work from home, which has become very popular most recently. Either way, a job is not your source of provision, or it should not be. God is our sole source of provision. He can use any means

PROSPERITY

He wills to supply the physical provision for us, such as income or products for life.

I heard a pastor say one time, "If you want to be healed, God has a billion ways to bring healing to your body. However, you only need one that is the best way to heal you." When I heard that, it resonated deep in my spirit. I have hung onto it since, especially during times I needed healing. Healing is only part of the provision which is provided to us from our Father God.

This can be applied to how God provides for our needs. Let's imagine that you are a doctor, and you know being a doctor is what you are called to do in life, everyday. You then are not called to be an accountant, an attorney, or a schoolteacher, but simply a doctor. This is also the avenue God will use to bless you, to fit you and be your source of income, provision or gain. As a doctor you can teach, or be a politician even, however, you were called to be a doctor so that is the source He will use to bless you.

Maybe a doctor also leases out rental houses, or a bed and breakfast as a second line of income. Deuteronomy 8: 18 says God gives us the power to obtain wealth. He has no money in heaven to send down to us when the bank account is getting low. Yet, He gifted the doctor with the understanding and wisdom to own rental houses with his inflow of gain from being a doctor originally. This is another way God blesses our lives and leads us to prosperity.

Deuteronomy 8:18 "And you shall remember the Lord your God, for it is He who gives you power to get wealth, that He may establish His covenant which He swore to your fathers, as it is this day."

Living in health in the body is a wealthy position to live in. In the same way living in financial gain is God's way of supporting His own. He wants us to experience prosperity. He has the perfect way for each one to do this too. Today, remember, there is only one provider, who is God. God can use many sources to provide fully for you, but you must take up the hoe and dig the source He provided to you, fertilize the ground He provided you, harvest the ground He provided to you. Trust Him because He knows best for you.

PRAYER

Thank you, Father, for the rich provisions in life You supply to us. We are truly grateful today and will take much care and wisdom in using these provisions to excel and flourish, our lives and Your Kingdom. This provision is part and parcel of Your salvation supplied to us while here on earth. Keep our eyes open to all the sources and veins of life-flowing provision You desire for us to use. Teach us to use this source of provision wisely and unselfishly, in the name of Jesus. Amen.

PROSPERITY

Day 7

Land

Leviticus 20:24 NKJV But I have said to you, "You shall inherit their land, and I will give it to you to possess, a land flowing with milk and honey." I am the Lord your God, who has separated you from the peoples.

Genesis 28:3-4 NKJV "May God Almighty bless you, and make you fruitful and multiply you, that you may be an assembly of peoples: and give you the blessing of Abraham, to you and your descendants with you, that you may inherit the land in which you are a stranger, which God gave to Abraham."

Psalm 37: 9, 29, 34 NKJV

9- For evildoers shall be cut off; but those who wait on the LORD, they shall inherit the earth.

29- The righteous shall inherit the land, and dwell in it forever.

34 – Wait on the Lord, and keep His way, and He shall exalt you to inherit the land; when the wicked are cut off, you shall see it.

37

PROSPERITY

When the writers of the Bible talked about 'land' they, many times referenced the concepts of power, self-sufficiency and especially legacy, or inheritance. These same concepts are represented likewise today regarding what owning land represents. The concept of ownership can be economic, or social in power. We look at land as a means to produce food, sustenance, or other assets to sell for money to apply to provisions in our living standards. Especially the assets a person cannot facilitate from being in a renter's position and living under the rules and boundaries of the landowner.

When I read about gaining land in scripture I also think about the other types of 'land' or foundational areas in my life, such as personal accomplishments and overcoming areas of void or lack in less physical terms. One of those areas could be becoming debt free, or learning how to paint and excel in it so well people want to buy your works of art. Another area of gaining land is when I have overcome an obstacle which had been a hinderance for months and finally gained ground to overcome that stumbling block, that also is gaining ground, or land. So, whether you're defeating a mountain of debt or walking through a valley of despair or purchasing a plot of land to plant fruit trees, gaining land is a big deal to God. He is a rewarder if you can make it a big deal to you too.

It is a true accomplishment if a person has 'moved up' a level in their life, it is being prosperous. Any type of acquiring land carries value and promise with it.

Land is truly provision. It's viewed that way in so many historic recounts in the Bible. This provision has stayed true and accurate for our day and time in history.

Go out today and conquer the land you're working to obtain in business, in the production of goods, or simply having the best manicured lawn on your block. It is all included in our blessing of God's provision.

PRAYER

Father, thank you for the land we have conquered so far and received provision with. We have a clear understanding this provision comes from and through You to us. We hold fast for further land that is to be possessed still, keeping our minds focused on the call, and being obedient to your word. We will be faithful to care for and maintain the provisions You have blessed us with now, knowing being the good and faithful servant, there is more to come, by being faithful with what we already have. You have a gracious, giving right hand and You are a bountiful supplier of our needs, as well as our desires. I pray we can be good stewards of all you have provided us with, in the name of Jesus I ask this. Amen.

PROSPERITY

Day 8

Solomon's Provision

Reading Reference

1 Kings 4: 7-34 NKJV Read the whole story but there are a couple key verses for today,

Key verse:

26- Solomon had forty thousand stalls of horses for his chariots, and twelve thousand horsemen. And these governors, each man in his month, provided food for King Solomon and for all who came to King Soloman's table. There was no lack in their supply.

29 – and God gave Solomon wisdom and exceedingly great understanding, and largeness of heart like the sand on the seashore.

A lesson we can take from Solomon's great success and provisions of wealth is what happened in his heart from substance misuse and overgrown pride. When he became king and further into his reign verse 29 says he had an exceedingly great understanding and largeness of heart. Sounds like the heart of God. It's possibly the type of compassion God has, so no wonder his provisions were so luxurious. When we have the heart of God, God can trust us with so much more.

Solomon did excellent things for God, such as building one of the most beautiful and richly decorated temples. It was Solomon's call to build the temple. We have already discussed the vast provision he experienced in 1 Kings 4: 7-34. Let's move forward to how Solomon handled his wealth and prosperity over time.

Beginning in Chapter **10 of 1 Kings, verse 24,**

Now all the earth sought the presence of Solomon to hear his wisdom, which God had put in his heart. Each man brought his present: articles of silver and gold, garments, armor, spices, horses, and mules, at a set rate year by year.

And Solomon gathered chariots and horsemen; he had one thousand four hundred chariots and twelve thousand horsemen, whom he stationed in the chariot cities and with the king at Jerusalem. The king made silver *as common* in Jerusalem as stones, and he made cedar trees as abundant as the sycamores which *are* in the lowland.

Also, Solomon had horses imported from Egypt and Keveh; the king's merchants bought them in Keveh at the *current* price. Now a chariot that was imported from Egypt cost six hundred *shekels* of silver, and a horse one hundred and fifty; and thus, through their agents, they exported *them* to all the kings of the Hittites and the kings of Syria.

Further in Chapter 11 the reason is given of why King Solomon's Kingdom was divided. 1Kings 11: 1-3 But King Solomon loved many foreign women, as well as the daughter of Pharaoh: women of the Moabites, Ammonites, Edomites, Sidonians, and Hittites—from the nations of whom the LORD had said to the children of Israel, "You shall not intermarry with them, nor they with you. Surely they will turn away your hearts after their gods." Solomon clung to these in love. And he had seven hundred wives, princesses, and three hundred concubines; and his wives turned away his heart.

Solomon directly disobeyed God. He married daughters of tribes that God said would pull Solomon away from Himself in worship, and into idol worship. The bigger issue was Solomon was aware who he should not marry, yet he married those women, and did not repent for clear disobedience of God's command. Maybe it was the fame, and money, or gold and gifts, and the admiration of the beautiful princesses from around the lands which swayed his heart more than God could.

I think though more than these simple things it was much more serious and the work of demons and evil spirits that he became entangled with via his wives, and the course pride. Pride of life caught his heart and the rebellion to his original calling grew. Eventually that call was forgotten. We don't know, we are only told in scripture it was this clear disobedience of marriages. However it happened, Solomon allowed the voices of his foreign wives to speak louder than the Lord's voice.

Idols moved into the beautiful temple created for the Lord God of Israel and God removed his hand of protection and provision from Solomon's life.

In history, even church history, this stumbling block has devoured many a just and prophetic voice of

power in the church. Notice it wasn't the great
amount of wealth and possessions, but the
connections and disregard to a direct boundary placed
in Solomon's life by God which he simply ignored.
Solomon's downfall, like so many others we see
today, was the result of a changed heart condition.
Maybe the heart condition came because of their
perspective of their gains, but God doesn't agree with
all cultures and the way they worship.

Here is something to remember, a person doesn't
have to be wealthy to acquire this deceptive mindset.
Some of the poorest people I have encountered in life
have the same pridefulness towards their only $50.00
as Solomon had about his 700 wives and over 300
concubines, not to mention the gold, silver and
luxuries which would today be worth billions.

How does this happen? Through the demonic spirit
called mammon. It can happen to anyone. It can
happen to poor people, it can happen to middle-class
people, and it can happen to wealthy people because
it happens in a person's heart, not their wallet.

How do we avoid this happening in our lives? One
way the bible teaches to combat this spirit is to cast
out the demon of mammon. Another way is, and
should be combined with the first way, by giving our
money and possessions to others. The bible teaches
through the act of giving and sowing the blessings of
God can financially prosper into the work of His
kingdom here on earth.

Along with those two weapons, is through constant
thankfulness to God. Keeping our focus on God as
the source of it, and not ourselves as the source of

our prosperity. Pride is sneaky however, and that spirit doesn't play fair with others.

Keep a keen, consistent eye on the planks in your life that want to glorify you. Always keep a giving mindset. Follow the instruction of the Lord with all the provisions He places in your hands. Use them wisely with a kingdom mindset. Let no physical, earthly thing come between you and God's relationship.

By using some of these boundaries as a guard, you give God the space to provide increase into your life, if that is what's part of His plan for you. It's about His kingdom, not yours.

Remember, it was the most beautiful, most talented, best dressed, most trusted angel who fell the quickest and hardest from Heaven.

PRAYER

Thank you, Lord, for all the perfect provision You have placed into my life. May I use what You have placed in my care wisely and for the good of the Kingdom. Keep my mindset on using this prosperity as a tool for You, and not only as a source of joy for myself. Help me to keep any idols from popping up; if they try, help me Holy Spirit to notice and act in my heart first, to stop the enemy from getting any of the precious gifts you have given to me. Continue to teach me what prosperity from God really is and how it is to work and glorify You. I ask these things in the name of Jesus. Amen.

PROSPERITY

CHAPTER 2

OUR FRUIT OF ENOUGH

Day 9

I AM is Enough

Reading Reference:

Matthew 6:31-34 NKJV "Therefore do not worry, saying, 'What shall we eat?' or 'What shall we drink?' or 'What shall we wear?' For after all these things the Gentiles seek. For your heavenly Father knows that you need all these things. But seek first the kingdom of God and His righteousness, and all these things shall be added to you. Therefore, do not worry about tomorrow, for tomorrow will worry about its own things. Sufficient for the day is its own trouble.

Everyday God is able, willing, to supply us with enough, and He always does for me. He does supply our needs. When we ask, He loves to supply our wants. The title of today's study is so vast a whole book can be written about how, I AM, is simply enough.

Typically, the verses from Matthew 6:31-34 talk about God's provision of our daily needs, especially verse 34. When I think of the word worry, I think of having anxiety about a situation, and it being stressful. But it also can be as simple as thinking about the situation a lot, thinking about the worst thing that

47

could happen in the situation, even if it doesn't cause anxiety, that also is still being worried.

These verses show us we serve a personal God. An all-knowing, all-understanding, ever-providing source in our life.

Are you resting today on His promise that we can trust Him, seek Him first when a situation comes up? We can trust Him every day not just for the simple things but for those things that we could choose to worry about. I know in the past trusting Him to give me the best advice, to show me the way to take in a difficult situation without worry has been a difficult thing to learn. If it is impossible in our minds to obtain, He is always enough. His desires and will for our life, for our tomorrows are enough.

Having enough can also mane having enough groceries for the week, having enough time to take the family to a restaurant on the spur of the moment or taking a family vacation. Having enough to me resembles prosperity quite frankly. I think this brings me to another point to consider; prosperity looks different to each of us. Each image of prosperity is correct because this is the desire the Lord has put in each heart to reflect. In any way you see prosperity, I AM is enough.

There are so many ways God is enough. Always remember when it comes to walking out today, He is enough, and His supply is enough.

PRAYER

Father, thank you for keeping superfluous expectations in check today. Keep before each of my thoughts throughout today all the ways You are enough for each need and want in this day. Help me live satisfied, mentally satisfied especially, in the understanding of I AM being all I need. May I live up to Your expectations and no one else's. Thank You Father for being my Provider.

PROSPERITY

Day 10

Enough for Kingdom Service

Reading Reference:

Exodus 36:1-7 NKJV

"And Bezalel and Aholiab, and every gifted artisan in whom the Lord has put wisdom and understanding, to know how to do all manner of work for the service of the sanctuary, shall do according to all that the Lord has commanded."

Then Moses called Bezalel and Aholiab, and every gifted artisan in whose heart the Lord had put wisdom, everyone whose heart was stirred, to come and do the work. And they received from Moses all the offering which the children of Israel had brought for the work of the service of making the sanctuary. So, they continued bringing to him freewill offerings every morning. Then all the craftsmen who were doing all the work of the sanctuary came, each from the work he was doing, and they spoke to Moses, saying, "The people bring much more than enough for the service of the work which the Lord commanded *us* to do."

So Moses gave a commandment, and they caused it to be proclaimed throughout the camp, saying, "Let neither man nor woman do any more work for the offering of the sanctuary." And the people were restrained from bringing, because the material they had was sufficient for all the work to be done—indeed too much.

We are given enough of anything we need to provide service in the Kingdom of God. We exist as more than enough for service in the kingdom working for God, as long as God has called us to that work. God provides us all we need to accomplish our work in His kingdom.

This story above of Moses and God's chosen people building the temple gives us a glimpse of what enough looks like. God's building wisdom and Moses' understanding of God' voice, provided the backdrop to the desires for the temple God had in mind. Eventually there is surplus, more than enough, was given to build this temple and Moses has to say to the people to stop bringing the gold and silver for building. This gives proof when we put the kingdom first, God always leaves a supply for our personal gain after.

I have heard so many Christians being negative about giving to churches, like our modern-day tabernacles to attend, and there is much criticism of lavish looking church buildings, and foyers, or social gathering areas at church and it just sounds weird to me how people would say those things! I would like to personally tell those who think like that, I and my husband have given to many areas in our church, to many renovations and upgrades to our church, and not one time has God left us lacking in what we need. The mindset of the church having too many nice things is just not on my radar, because I know what kind of God I serve. It honors God for His house to look beautiful and comfortable, and out of the gratefulness in my heart for everything God has done for me, I will honor Him, by honoring His house, and by honoring His ministers. I realize my body is also His temple, but my church building is a testament of how good God is to me. I simply enjoy giving back to God of the goodness of his bountifulness to me and being able to sit in air conditioning that works when I go to church.

Notice it says in Exodus 36:2 everyman brought because they were stirred up in their hearts. The Lord knew who had what and could make specific skilled items and He moved upon those people to bring those things specifically for the Kingdom work. The point is, be led in what you give, but what you are led to do, absolutely do!

Verse 7 in our text says the stuff they had and brought was sufficient for all that needed to be accomplished, and there was too much. God is a too much God! We think with earthly limitations, but not God. He has placed this surplus inside each of us to be used exactly for a specific kingdom work.

By being led to move and do your part in giving to building the kingdom means no gift is too small.

PRAYER

Father, show me new ways I can add to Your kingdom. Rush ideas and creations through me so as to add to Your plans and Your desires for Your kingdom. Thank you for making this possible for me to do, for making my gifts enough to serve, and providing back more than enough for life. It is an honor to support and flourish Your Kingdoms work here on earth!

Day 11
We have Been Made Enough

Reading Reference

Psalms 23

The Lord is my Shepherd; I shall not want. He makes me to lie down in green pastures; He leads me beside the still waters. He restores my soul; He leads me in the paths of righteousness for His name's sake. Yea, though I walk through the valley of the shadow of death, I will fear no evil; For You are with me; Your rod and Your staff, they comfort me. You prepare a table before me in the presence of my enemies; You anoint my head with oil; My cup runs over. Surely goodness and mercy shall follow me all the days of my life; and I will dwell in the house of the LORD forever.

I recently learned a foundational truth about the 23rd Psalms that has changed my perspective on being enough through Jesus.

Verse 1 in the Psalm states it outright and simply, if I keep the Lord is my Shephard, I shall not want. This is now my favorite verse of the Bible. It says, I will have and am now experiencing enough. He goes on the next few verses to explain the way we have enough in Jesus, our Shepherd. This verse tells me; I want nothing bad or hurtful either. At one time I fought day after day with a food addiction. Addiction is a want. An unfulfilled longing for something I think I must have. Verse 1 says to me, I don't live with any addiction…there is no wanting the drug, no wanting the food, no wanting the money to gamble. Because I follow Him as my personal Shepherd, I shall not want. I will not want. I do not want out of the disease of addiction. That is powerful!

That isn't all, verse 2 says, 'He makes me to lie down in green pastures;' As a Western thinking Christian I have always pictured lush grass, green and long for as far as my eye could see. Like some of the manicured lawns we see in America. Rolling hills of alfalfa grass are beautifully watered and lusciously green because of health and vitality of being nourished. That to me would be any sheep's perfect pasture full of abundance. I thank the Lord every day for correcting my understanding of this image.

David wrote this. The same David who spent years and years shepherding sheep in the hills of Israel. My image of lush grass is incorrect. I wasn't seeing this verse from David's perspective of what the rolling hills are like in Israel. David moved his sheep up and over a rigid, rocky terrain along mountains and cliffs, literally called 'green pastures' [1] in his day.

There was nothing lush about feeding his sheep here. There was a wind though, which would catch the moisture from the sea in its breeze. Those breezes would then collide with the mountains and provide just enough moisture to grow a little green grass here and there in spots under rocks, along the mountains. Fresh green springs of grass for the wondering shepherds to search out and find for their flock of sheep. This gave the sheep their days' nourishment and sustenance for life.

It was the shepherd, like David, who needed watchful eyes to lead his flock to the freshly sprouted greens each day. The sheep would nibble down everything green to where only the rocks were left along the mountains, and they would then rest, and the next day move on to find that day's sustenance.

The shepherd was moving and searching each day, considering the sheep he was responsible for, considering each need they had, while also protecting them as they followed him. The sheep in turn trusted he would provide enough for that day.

This new image was powerful. It showed me sheep might get fat and lazy in a field that was Americanized and full, why go anywhere. Why move through the mountains of life, trusting the Shephard if I could just lay in one place, eat a little over here and just roll my head over to eat more grass later. That is self-sustaining. That is the Western mindset. Sometimes its good to be in a place where we must trust the Shephard to find our best work for the day. The Shephard knows where my nourishment lays; He knows how to provide my portion from his hand. My needs are at the forefront of His eyes. He is the God who sees, He is the God of enough.

My daily nourishment is found in listening for the Shephard to call me and provide the sustenance of

PROSPERITY

His Word, of His company, of His will to me for the
day. I shall not want. It is vital to listen for His voice
of instruction, but it's even more vital that I go when
He beckons me it's time to eat.

My vitality depends on listening for His voice.

PRAYER

Father, help me trust Your calling and preparation
of the green pastures You have perfectly placed in my
path today. May I never get ahead of Your green
pastures for my own fulfillment and lose track of
Your sufficient provision of my daily needs. I will fear
no evil thing as You lead, I have no want as long as
my trust is in You. Thank you for being the God of
enough. Amen.

Day 12

Being Kind is a Gift

Reading Reference:

Proverbs 31:26 NKJV She opens her mouth with wisdom, and on her tongue is the law of kindness.

Ephesians 4:32 NKJV And be kind to one another, tenderhearted, forgiving one another, even as God in Christ forgave you.

Jesus the Christ is our established example of how kindness is a gift. Jesus was the best gift. His fruit of kindness was stunning. He was kind enough to look over the sinful nature and redeem us out of that nature forever. He had the kindness to see past sin, into a precious place He only knows. He didn't have to, He chose to.

Often the statement is said, "He or she did_____ out of the kindness of their heart." This is the gift Christ has given to mankind by no mistake of choice. Kindness was purposefully created by God to be placed back on earth by the gift of Christ's life on earth, then death and resurrection. In that process He sealed our fate forever.

I have often heard another statement, 'it costs you nothing to be kind,' but I want to remind you it did cost God something. The price Jesus paid, we didn't

PROSPERITY

pay. The honor of bestowing kindness especially towards the undeserving is precious, a priceless gift God expects us to use daily, if we have received the same from Him.

Today the lesson is simple, yet the fruit of kindness is a sweet substance. If you are in Christ, and He is in you, you have all the skill you need to show kindness. Oh, don't we need this kindness today. Reflect on the kindness of Jesus' actions as you read through scripture.

PRAYER

Father, show us each the opportunity to share the fruit of kindness in our day-to-day encounters. Especially with other Christians, but also towards those who don't know You yet, and can be refreshed by the sweet fruit of kindness. May we touch those who have gotten the wrong impression of Your desire for us, to live in us and dwell close by through salvation. The one with a disappointment in the Christians theology by a misrepresentation in behavior from a hurting Christian they had met. I pray the kindness of Jesus will leak out of my choices and decisions, and conversation with the lost, and the wondering. I ask this in Jesus' name. Amen

Day 13

Jesus' Fruit of Giving Gifts as Our Example of Giving

Reading Reference

Titus 3:3-7 NKJV For we ourselves were also once foolish, disobedient, deceived, serving various lusts and pleasures, living in malice and envy, hateful and hating one another. But when the kindness and the love of God our Savior toward man appeared, not by works of righteousness which we have done, but according to His mercy He saved us, through the washing of regeneration and renewing of the Holy Spirit, whom He poured out on us abundantly through Jesus Christ our Savior, that having been justified by His grace we should become heirs according to the hope of eternal life.

I am a natural gift giver, but I wasn't always so willing to give. Over time, after becoming saved this trait began to be in operation more and more. It began with giving tithe and offerings in church.

Compassion for other people's needs began to be important. Interestingly, the more I used my own

PROSPERITY

surplus and resources to give to other people. God Himself continuously supplied my own needs, above and beyond with very little effort of my own in prayer or supplications. God is a natural giver. He is the original Giver of gifts.

Why? I think it is because the giving of gifts to His children is a very high priority of His nature. I began getting nice gifts like, watches, money, and opportunity as God only knew I desired. God gives to the givers, it's just that simple. Gift giving is His idea and once we conform to His nature, we naturally become His very nature. Our goal as Christians is simply to replicate Christ and His desires.

The main thought to take with you today is, God gives to the givers. Practice the art of gift giving. Practice being led, specifically, listening to Him, kind of giving to others. Give especially to those in the household of faith. Galatians 6:10, Therefore, as we have opportunity, let us do good to all, especially to those who are of the household of faith.

PRAYER

Father God, I pray that I and those reading this prayer will merge so perfectly into the image of Your will we cannot be separated from Your true reflection in our giving gifts. Help us to see new ways to give, and with the courage and trust in You to supplement our giving to others. May our gifts reflect Your love for those we live around every day. May your reflection spill over to those we don't know as we pass them in the stores, or on the streets. Help us to produce a true honest image of Christ through a growing fruit of gift giving.

Day 14

Jesus & Holy Spirit are Our Gifts from God

Reading Reference

Romans 14:17 NKJV For the kingdom of God is not eating and drinking, but righteousness and peace and joy in the Holy Spirit.

John 20:22 NKJV And when He had said this, He breathed on them, and said to them, 'Receive the Holy Spirit.'

2 Corinthians 13:14 NKJV The grace of the Lord Jesus Christ, and the love of God, and the communion of the Holy Spirit be with you all. Amen.

Acts 15:8 NKJV So God, who knows the heart, acknowledged them by giving them the Holy Spirit, just as He did to us, (more?)

Luke 11:13 NKJV "If you then, being evil, know how to give good gifts to your children, how much more will your heavenly Father give the Holy Spirit to those who ask Him!"

John 1:14 NKJV And the Word became flesh and dwelt among us, and we beheld His glory, the glory as of the only begotten of the Father, full of grace and truth.

The person of the Holy Spirit is truly a gift to the church, from the beginning of time. He is a valuable and needed gift to myself in so many ways.

We can live a full and blessed life by our communication and submission to His advice and suggestions daily. There are many things I would have missed or gotten wrong without the leading of Holy Spirit in my life.

Following the directive from the Holy Spirit will keep from needing a miracle in life, He can keep us living in the blessing provided by Jesus.

I have recently learned receiving a miracle means we somehow came into a crisis. So, receiving a miracle of some types isn't the same as being blessed. The Holy Spirit is the One we can counsel with when we need advice or understanding. He is an excellent listener, understanding our bare motives deep in our hearts. We can't make a decision, openly or silently, without the Holy Spirit seeing it and knowing it fully.

Holy Spirit is the part of God, Himself who dwells inside us once saved. He is our nearest counselor, our truest Confidant when distress comes. He is the Wisdom of God as a part of God, given to guide and warn us in times of need. When we learn to listen and yield to Him, we can help others when they need us too.

God intended His only Son, Jesus, to be the ultimate gift to us. As the direct image of God, He embodied full grace for all that had come undone on the earth and He provided the absolute truth that could get us back on course with living a blessed life. The life He intended Adam and Eve to live out fully.

I am not referring to 'my truth' or 'your truth.' This absolute truth as what Jesus embodies. The other claims of truth are counterfeit and weak in their very foundations, leaving them as vapors of mere opinion dressed up as trickery to diffuse absolute truth. Absolute truth is not personal or derived from people. It is actually solid, unmovable, uncompromisable and offensive to the non-surrendered mind. It looks a lot like the rumors the Devil spread across the Heavens to convince one-third of all the angels, God's own servants, to follow him, instead of God.

By the grace that accompanies this truth we can reveal 'our truth' with the pure unfiltered, life-changing truth from the Ultimate Gift God sent to us. The Gift that wholly redeems.

Jesus was God's ultimate Gift. Paying the ultimate price for all of us. If it wasn't for this Gift, we would have very different lives.

Search no more for through as Jesus, Our Ultimate Gift, is available to all.

PRAYER

Father, help us to fully receive this Ultimate Gift from You. This Gift who provides full grace for the redemption of our futures. No matter what our pasts know about us, we can all receive fully of this Gift. This grace covers and restores that history to peace with You. May we also fully receive the truth, in each regard, for the edification of our minds and desires. Help us honestly give this beautiful gift to those who haven't experienced it in all its weight and glory yet. I ask this in the precious name of Jesus, Amen.

Day 15

Our Talents Are Gifts

Reading Reference:

Matthew 25:14-30 NKJV

The Parable of the Talents

"For *the kingdom of heaven is* like a man traveling to a far country, *who* called his own servants and delivered his goods to them. And to one he gave five talents, to another two, and to another one, to each according to his own ability; and immediately he went on a journey. Then he who had received the five talents went and traded with them, and made another five talents. And likewise he who *had received* two gained two more also. But he who had received one went and dug in the ground, and hid his lord's money. After a long time the lord of those servants came and settled accounts with them.

"So he who had received five talents came and brought five other talents, saying, 'Lord, you delivered to me five talents; look, I have gained five more talents besides them.' His lord said to him, 'Well *done,* good and faithful servant; you were faithful over a few things, I will make you a ruler over many things. Enter into the joy of your lord.' He also who had received two talents came and said, 'Lord, you

delivered to me two talents; look, I have gained two
more talents besides them.' His lord said to
him, 'Well *done,* good and faithful servant; you have
been faithful over a few things, I will make you ruler
over many things. Enter into the joy of your lord.'

"Then he who had received the one talent came and
said, 'Lord, I knew you to be a hard man, reaping
where you have not sown, and gathering where you
have not scattered seed. And I was afraid, and went
and hid your talent in the ground. Look, *there* you
have *what is* yours.'

"But his lord answered and said to him, 'You wicked
and lazy servant, you knew that I reap where I have
not sown, and gather where I have not scattered
seed. So you ought to have deposited my money with
the bankers, and at my coming I would have received
back my own with interest. So take the talent from
him, and give *it* to him who has ten talents.

'For to everyone who has, more will be given, and he
will have abundance; but from him who does not
have, even what he has will be taken away. And cast
the unprofitable servant into the outer
darkness. There will be weeping and gnashing of
teeth.'

Matthew 25:25 NKJV And I was afraid and went
and hid your talent in the ground. Look, there you
have what is yours.

Two things go through my mind when I read this
verse. The first thing is fear came into the heart of
this servant when given his talent. Yet in the Bible, we
68

are told 365 times, "do not fear, do not be afraid, (Gatlin)." [2] Why then are we apprehensive or fearful when we should have full confidence of no fear? Have you ever been given a gift, and also been afraid to use it, or touch it? I think I have a couple times so I can relate to this person in verse 25, who was just afraid to do something wrong, that they did nothing at all. Laid the talent aside, as too precious to experience, and thereby lost out.

Second, it can be seen by the last statement in the verse that the servant never really received the gift as their own. Some gifts cannot be seen or received until the person receives salvation. This is similar to what happened to me. I never played an instrument, yet the music was so special, and I just thought I enjoyed music. However, very soon after I was saved, I began playing drums, learning music theory and jumping right into worship at church. I know I was meant to play drums, it's obvious, but the desire was not born until after I was saved. I played in many churches and Christian venues, in front of a few people as well as in front to vast crowds and on tv. But I stepped into that gift once I noticed my desire for it. I was 35 years old when I began playing drums. I use this example because it is never too late to begin using a talent for the Lord.

Maybe the talent was complicated, too big for the servants' expectations of his own life. Maybe the talent was possibly offensive to the servant, maybe below the servants' standards and an offense that he would be regarded and chosen for the executor of the talent.

PROSPERITY

What have any of us done in the past when we are hurt or offended about something in our lives? We hide it of course. We don't want to admit the offense exists. We also don't attach any of our identity with the substance of the offense. We are even ready to quickly return it to its rightful owners. I have been guilty of this and have had to repent for my rejection of the talent.

If we could see that our talents don't define us, but that we can define our talents, maybe they can then be the useful gift they were intended to be. The God-given gifts can also be seen in the lives of the unsaved, such as singers, bands, artists, speakers, businessmen who are all very talented yet unsaved. We can observe their 'possible place' in the kingdom from what they do on earth.

PRAYER

Father, help us to see our talents and gifts for the body as valuable and pleasing to You. Help us to understand You see them as valuable and important to Your kingdom. Help us to truly explore each one and give us the opportunity to bless you with each one in return for the gift.

CHAPTER 4

OUR FRUIT OF ABUNDANCE

PROSPERITY

Day 16

Freedom in Abundance

Reading Reference:

Matthew 25:29 NKJV For to everyone who has, more will be given, and he will have abundance; but from him who does not have, even what he has will be taken away.

Matthew 13:12 NKJV For whoever has, to him more will be given, and he will have abundance; but whoever does not have, even what he has will be taken away from him.

2 Corinthians 8: 1-15 NKJV

Moreover, brethren, we make known to you the grace of God bestowed on the churches of Macedonia: that in a great trial of affliction the abundance of their joy and their deep poverty abounded in the riches of their liberality. For I bear witness that according to *their* ability, yes, and beyond *their* ability, *they were* freely willing, imploring us with much urgency that we would receive the gift and the fellowship of the ministering to the saints. And not *only* as we had hoped, but they first gave themselves to the Lord, and *then* to us by the will of God. So we urged Titus, that as he had begun, so he

PROSPERITY

would also complete this grace in you as well. But
as you abound in everything—in faith, in speech, in
knowledge, in all diligence, and in your love for us,
that you abound in this grace also.

I speak not by commandment, but I am testing the
sincerity of your love by the diligence of others. For
you know the grace of our Lord Jesus Christ, that
though He was rich, yet for your sakes He became
poor, that you through His poverty might
become rich.

And in this I give advice: It is to your advantage not
only to be doing what you began and were desiring to
do a year ago; but now you also must complete the
doing *of it;* that as *there was* a readiness to
desire *it,* so *there* also *may be* a completion out of
what *you* have. For if there is first a willing mind, *it
is* accepted according to what one has, *and* not
according to what he does not have.

For *I do* not *mean* that others should be eased and you
burdened; but by an equality, *that* now at this time
your abundance *may supply* their lack, that their
abundance also may *supply* your lack—that there may
be equality. As it is written, "He who *gathered* much
had nothing left over, and he who *gathered* little had no
lack."

Greed or fear are not traits that will allow
abundance to flourish in our future. 2 Corinthians12
gives a key to continued abundance and that desire.
Abundance starts with being excited to give. Being
selfless and looking for opportunities to fill a void in
someone else's life. Filling needs anonymous is even
better.

74

Our Fruit of Christianity

There was a season in my life when I began to crochet little quick accessories like scarves. I wore one that was made with sparkle yarn and made into cute little snowflake shapes all down the sides of the scarf. The snowflakes were free flowing, almost hanging and this made the little flakes sparkle because of the shinny part of the specialized yarn. A lady who I know doesn't crochet made genuine complements about the scarf and I knew in my heart it delighted her. In that very moment the scarf became hers. One, I can make another one, and she doesn't crochet at all. Second, I wanted her heart to be clear of coveting, and well knowing God can teach her about the issues of coveting in His time. I wasn't about to let her trip over some scarf.

I took it off my neck and blessed her with my brand new, straight off the Saturday night hook, scarf, which I also really liked as well. It was such a joyful experience, and I know I would do it again.

I did too. On another Sunday at church, I had just purchased this beautiful red leather purse for the Christmas season. After a sister at church almost drooled all over that purse, I found a plastic shopping bag and I emptied all my possessions out of that purse and into the shopping bag. I gifted that beautiful bag to her, on the spot with zero remorse, and only allowed my eye to linger on its leaving for a few seconds. It was a beautiful purse; I fully planned on keeping the entire Christmas season. I can tell you; I have been blessed to have some of the most beautiful purses since that day, and only a few of them did I pay for.

PROSPERITY

There is a character of God, and the way He gives that I enjoy emulating. All abundance comes from God. He is our source. It is our job to be His storehouse, willing to supply, knowing we will have an abundant flow back from Him, for all of our needs, and our desires as long as we seek Him and His kingdom first.

PRAYER

Father, I know of Your goodness, and Your plenty. Thank you for being the example we can follow in giving out of our abundance and storehouse. Thank you also for that special freedom that comes when we hold nothing back from giving to our brothers and sisters. Lead me in more ways I can give and be a supply to those who may not even necessarily need the things I have but that they just really enjoy them. I ask that as long as I have the supply to give, You will show me where those supplies can be used. I ask this in the name of Jesus, who supplied His own life, for my own. Amen.

Day 17

Abundance from God

Reading Reference:

2 Chronicles 17:3-6 NKJV Now the Lord was with Jehoshaphat, because he walked in the former ways of his father David; he did not seek the Baals, but sought the God of his father, and walked in His commandments and not according to the acts of Israel. Therefore, the Lord established the kingdom in his hand; and all Judah gave presents to Jehoshaphat, and he had riches and honor in abundance. And his heart took delight in the ways of the Lord; moreover he removed the high places and wooden images from Judah.

Nehemiah 9:21 NKJV Forty years You sustained them in the wilderness; they lacked nothing; their clothes did not wear out and their feet did not swell.

John 10:10 NKJV The thief does not come except to steak, and to kill, and to destroy. I have come that they may have life, and that they may have it more abundantly.

PROSPERITY

The word abundance in Strong's Concordance; pĕrissŏs #4053.[3] Strong's describe abundance as Superabundance (in quantity) or superior (in quality), excessive, overflowing, surplus, over and above, more than enough, profuse, extraordinary, above the ordinary, more than sufficient.

John 10:10 says we may have life more abundantly because of knowing and living for God. Scripture compares the two lifestyles, one without God's abundant provisions and the other lifestyle we are promised in God.

We each live according to the abundance we can believe for. Since God's provision is promised as being profuse and excessive, if we aren't seeing that in any particular area in our lives, it isn't because the promise doesn't work. It's just time to shift gears of our expectation of abundance.

The bible is stable and sure, full of truth, and like God Himself it cannot be untrue or having lies. If there is a lack of some kind it is coming from my end, not from the source, or God.

I do believe once we understand how to receive abundant life from God, and especially how to use that abundance correctly, God will undoubtedly continue to supply more and more even overflowing and more than sufficient.

God is a practical God, very dependable and follows His own traditional ways. He is steady and doesn't waver, nor changed from doing things the way He has laid out in the Old Testament. His reflections of

78

abundance can be seen throughout the Old Testaments rituals and celebrations. We now have even a better covenant than they had, yet we can depend on His follow through to be almost identical. I encourage you to search the history in the Old Testament about the abundance of God.

PRAYER

Father, I think You, that You are my source, and You enrich my life abundantly. Teach me to be able to observe and respect what the many things are You do throughout my life. Thank You for being my source and provider. Keep me once again today in your promise of abundance. Amen.

PROSPERITY

Day 18

The Heart Speaks Abundance

Reading Reference:

Luke 6:45 NKJV A good man out of the good treasure of his heart brings forth good; and an evil man out of the evil treasure of his heart brings forth evil. For out of the abundance of the heart the mouth speaks.

What needs to be understood first about the verse in Luke 6, is that is it written to Christ followers. Abundance can go two ways Luke 6 says. This is important to know about the condition of our hearts. We can hold an evil treasure, or we can hold a good treasure. Either way, our heart will expose the type of treasure we carry around. It is up to us to fill our hearts with one or the other, good treasure or evil treasure.

It's impossible to blame God when our life isn't producing abundance because as we see this comes from the storage unit of our heart. Prosperity and abundance have already been provided and waiting for us to retrieve it from our source, God. His work is finished. This work was finished on the cross.

No one enjoys going through the avoided closet where all the random things we don't know what to do with getting stuffed over time. Maybe it's time to rummage through your treasures and remove any toys of unforgiveness and bitterness which are very common obstacles of an evil treasure. Each treasure can be different for everyone, but no matter what is kept there, it's time to clear out and replace the things that hinder our testimony as a Christian. Evil treasures are not a good or true representation of a child of God.

We are each responsible for the continuous cleaning of the soil in our hearts. Abundance is like farming. The crop depends on the health of the soil, the quality of the seed we plant. Seeds of offense, if not dug up quickly can overtake the whole harvest like weeds do. If the crop isn't tended to regularly by the time for harvest in autumn, you can lose quite a bit of good fruit.

Make up your mind today to finally clean the house and weed your garden. This way abundance can grow freely.

PRAYER

Father, today as I examine the treasures lying around in my heart, help me to pluck out the items that don't project true Christlikeness and true living. I pray I will honestly lay out all that I have before you and remove fully those things which cannot give you glory. Thank You Lord for your work in me. Amen.

Day 19

Old Testament Forms of Abundance

Reading Reference:

PEACE

Psalm 37:11 NKJV But the meek shall inherit the earth and shall delight themselves in the abundance of peace.

DAILY NEEDS

Deuteronomy 26:15 NKJV Look down from Your holy habitation, from heaven, and bless Your people Israel and the land which You have given us, just as You swore to our fathers, "a land flowing with milk and honey."

SECURITY

Deuteronomy 8:18 NKJV "And you shall remember the Lord your God, for it is He who give you power to get wealth, that He may establish His covenant which He swore to your fathers, as it is this day.

Peace could possibly be the most precious gift of abundance from God, outside of our salvation itself.

PROSPERITY

The Bible references God's abundant peace, throughout the Word. It's a good time spent to go through and find all the ways He provides peace.

Just before my mother's transition to heaven last year, I was experiencing a very difficult time where during that time only God's peace could get me through it. God gave me such a profound, deep and enduring type of peace. He used the verses in 1 Thessalonians 4: 10b-14 which says, "...But we urge you, brethren, that you increase more and more; that you also aspire to lead a quiet life, to mind your own business, and to work with your own hands, as we commanded you, that you may walk properly toward those who are outside, and *that* you may lack nothing.

But I do not want you to be ignorant, brethren, concerning those who have fallen asleep, lest you sorrow as others who have no hope. For if we believe that Jesus died and rose again, even so God will bring with Him those who sleep in Jesus."

The grief of my mom passing on turned to peace and a simple knowing and trusting in the abundance of peace the Old and New testament speaks of when a parent passes away. It can be such a hard time without the promises of God. We will see our families and loving friends who have passed before us IF each of us are going to Heaven. It's a promise in scripture. The verses tell us not to be sad and grieve like those who are perishing and have no hope or promise of this kind. There was a profound peace that came with this understanding during the passing of my mother. It was such reassurance of God loving His own, even past death. We have no fear of death because of this promise.

Security is also a good form of abundance and gift from God. This isn't only our safety day by day as we maneuver through life. It also includes the security of our inheritance and our salvation. I am very grateful for the security in Christ. Finding our security in Christ is keep our focus on righteousness. Jesus paid a heavy price to make us righteous, so don't let anyone convince you, you are not what Jesus paid for.

Another abundant gift mentioned throughout the old, and new, testament is the wonderful and perfect way Father God provides for those who are His own. God does this by so many different resources. A main resource He uses is His Church's body. He moves money through the hands of the people in His church. I desire to be a source out to a brother or sister for assistance in need! If we love the brethren, we help supply their needs.

PRAYER

Father, show me through Your Word all the ways You provide super abounding supply to us Your children. Thank you for this abundance, I do not take it lightly or flippantly. Show to me all You have supplied for my life so that I may be a valuable testimony to Your goodness, and a quality reflection of who You are.

PROSPERITY

Day 20

New Testament Forms of Abundance

WISDOM

2 Corinthians 2:4, 12:7 NKJV

4—For out of much affliction and anguish of heart I wrote to you, with many tears, not that you should be grieved, but that you might know the love which I have so abundantly for you.

7—And lest I should be exalted above measure by the abundance of the revelations, a thorn in the flesh was given to me, a messenger of Satan to buffet me, lest I be exalted above measure.

LIFE

John 10:10 NKJV The thief does not come except to steal, and to kill, and to destroy. I have come that they may have life, and that they may have it more abundantly.

MERCY & HOPE

1 Peter 1: 3-5 NKJV Blessed be the God and Father of our Lord Jesus Christ, who according to His abundant mercy has begotten us again to a living hope through the resurrection of Jesus Christ from the dead, to an inheritance incorruptible and undefiled and that does not fade away, reserved in heaven for you, who are kept by the power of God through faith for salvation ready to be revealed in the last time.

Wisdom supplied by God is a valuable item to house in our hearts. It connects to living abundantly in every area of our lives, with joy, completeness, and complements. I have mentioned before that wisdom is not knowledge, but wisdom is the understanding of what to do, and how to flourish with the knowledge we are given.

It is through wisdom we are able to love those around us in the way God has asked us to. Love gives us the ability to cover the tender things for God's healing touch, as well as exposing the tough things that no longer match our new character in Christ.

Mercy and hope are valuable treasures that could make life hard without them. I know I could not think on these things I speak of without the power filled mercy God has given me. Nor could I look forward to His continued work in my life without the hope for the things which I cannot see with my physical eyes as of yet. There are many things I am believing God for, and I know He is faithful.

God desires us to live life fully here, and not just wait for the life we will live in heaven. He provides good things in this life, while we are still on earth, which He separated out for us in John 10:10 from the things the enemy will bring into our lives. Abundance is one of the many good things God desires we experience. It is through abundance we help and give of the ones we see need things that we may have available. Someone living in poverty isn't available to give to those in need. Which is why I can't wrap my mind around so many in the church today who are vehemently speaking against prosperity! Then they contrast what they say by having jobs, and nice cars, or houses, or they appreciate those things at least.

Gifts in the church come in all various ways. Especially pastors, teachers and such. However, there are numerous other resources in the church we tend to forget, such as wise financial businessmen and women, lawyers, doctors, plumbers and various craftsmen. What I know of my resource, I am more than willing to offer that service and source out to a brother or sister for their prosperity in life.

I also think in the verse in 3 John 2 NKJV, which says, Beloved I pray that you may prosper in all things and be in health, just as your soul prospers. God desires our souls, the mind, will, and emotions part of us to prosper fully. In all things, we have the capacity to prosper according to this verse. All things include health, money, our bank accounts, our homes, having children, having grandchildren and living fully and with long life with our spouse. He doesn't put a limit on these things. I know so many of us do however, God doesn't. I believe if He can trust you with it, He will see that you have the opportunity to grab a hold of it. To live the abundant life now, on earth, as it is in Heaven.

PROSPERITY

Seek His word and find for yourself the different degrees of abundance God has already placed on His dinner table. He has laid each treasure out beautifully for our full consumption and use.

PRAYER

Father, thank You for the abundance that comes only from You. The abundance is satisfying and true. May I never forget it is from You, and that it is You who gives our family its abundance. Help us to remember abundance is not only about money, but how money can truly testify of You to the unsaved. I ask these things in the name of Jesus, Amen.

CHAPTER 5

OUR FRUIT OF MONEY

PROSPERITY

Day 21

We are Not Measured by Money

Reading Reference:

Acts 8:18-20 NKJV And when Simon saw that through the laying on of the apostles' hands the Holy Spirit was given, he offered them money, saying, "Give me this power also, that anyone on whom I lay hands may receive the Holy Spirit."

But Peter said to him, "Your money perish with you, because you thought that the gift of God could be purchased with money!

I Peter 1:18 NKJV And if you call on the Father, who without partiality judges according to each one's work, conduct yourselves throughout the time of your stay here in fear; knowing that you were not redeemed with corruptible things, like silver or gold, from your aimless conduct received by tradition from your fathers, but with the precious blood of Christ, as of a lamb without blemish and without spot. He indeed was foreordained before the foundation of the world, but was manifest in these last times for you who through Him believe in God who raised Him from the dead and give Him glory, so that your faith and hope are in God.

The story of Moses come to mind when I think about not being qualified or measured by the amount of money we have but by God's grace and mercy for our lives.

First, when Moses was born, he wasn't wealthy, his parents were slaves in a foreign country. But he was adopted by the pharaohs' sister, in the most prestigious home in the country of Egypt. He grew up royalty with not just money, but a line of power. As an adult through some unfortunate circumstances, he was suddenly outcast and desolate in the middle of a desert, stripped of all his royal prosperity. God still intervened during his next broke and desperate season and raised him up for his use, one of the greatest moves of God in all history, which was the removing of God's people, His heritage, from the bondages they lived under in Egypt, his homeland. Remember, God's people were the people his adopted family owned.

The story of Moses is found in Exodus 1:15 – Exodus 4:23. The story does not stop in Exodus 4, but his calling and direction is the focus in that set of scriptures.

Second, and the main idea to remember today about this story is God provided completely for him all his life. God provided for his call and assignment at birth, not because he had or did not have money. God provides not out of partiality, as stated in 1 Peter 1, but according to each one's work, what we may call, our calling from God. God will provide what you need to fulfill His calling on your life. Just like God provided for Jesus, in all the many ways He did, while Jesus was working out His own assigned ministry on earth. Jesus lacked nothing and taught that we also will have no lack.

PRAYER

Father, today in my journey, give me insight in my finances and how to grow them from here. Keep my steps pure as I move along fulfilling the call You placed on my life. I'm trusting in Your faithfulness and Word, remembering how You provided for Moses, and the disciples, and Jesus. I trust You, and I know my family is not alone, You have a plan, and purpose for our lives. You want us never lacking in money or income and resources. Show us a "more excellent way," in the name of Jesus. Amen

PROSPERITY

Day 22

Money is Only a Resource

Reading Reference:

Ecclesiastes 7:12 NKJV for wisdom is a defense as money is a defense, but the excellence of knowledge is that wisdom gives life to those who have it.

Ecclesiastes 10:19 NKJV A feast is made for laughter, and wine makes merry; but money answers everything.

Matthew 23:17 NKJV Fools and blind! For which is greater, the gold or the temple that sanctifies the gold?

1 Peter 3:3-4 NKJV Do not let your adornment be merely outward—arranging the hair, wearing gold, or putting on fine apparel – rather let it be the hidden person of the heart, with the incorruptible beauty of a gentle and quiet spirit, which is very precious in the sight of God.

Luke 22: 35-38 NKJV And He said to them, "When I sent you without money bag, knapsack, and sandals, did you lack anything? So they said, "Nothing."

PROSPERITY

Then He said to them, "But now, he who has a money bag, let him take it, and likewise a knapsack; and he who has no sword, let him sell his garment and buy one. For I say to you that this which is written must still be accomplished in Me: And He was numbered with the transgressors. "For the things concerning Me have an end." So they said, "Lord, look, here are two swords." And He said to them, "It is enough."

These scriptures referring to money, or gold, which represents wealth, but they mention keys in keeping the attitude about money in balance. Each scripture explains and warns believers how money can throw us off track if we see it any differently than that of a tool.

When I think of resources I think of tools and useful items to help accomplish a larger task. A hammer or nail gun helps the builder construct a home. A car helps people go from one place to the next- no matter the distance involved. A table is used to hold items for people to eat on, to write on, or have very important meetings at.

Money must be regarded the same way as it's useful for the purchase of a hammer, a car and a table. Money is used to spread the gospel, but it's not to be the gospel.

One important representation money takes on is supply for local churches. Tithe is both a tool and a mindset. As a tool it keeps the lights on in the sanctuary and the air conditioner running so in July, we can be comfortable while having the Word taught to us.

98

As a mindset, money represents thankfulness and honor towards God's gracious giving and supply into our lives. Gratitude for living in the blessing only He can provide is another reason for giving tithes. Not an exchange FOR the blessing, but because of what He has accomplished in our lives, giving that back towards Him for His blessing.

Luke 22 tells me when God sends me somewhere, I will lack nothing I need while doing His business. His disciples were sent out to minister the gospel into the streets and they were told not to take the money bags, and yet they answered Him how they were fully provided for. I am pretty sure that the word nothing means exactly 'no-thing' in the Greek, in the Hebrew, and in English. God is a trustworthy God!

PRAYER

Father, show me the clear direction You have for my future. If I am not going in that direction today, forgive me for not stopping to listen long enough, and for not being obedient, or having my own agenda before Yours. Turn my heart into the right direction toward Your goal. In the name of Jesus, I pray this request be fulfilled. Amen.

PROSPERITY

Day 23

One of God's Blessings is Money

Reading Reference:

Psalm 112:1-3 NKJV Praise the Lord! Blessed is the man who fears the LORD, who delights greatly in His commandments. His descendants will be mighty on earth; the generation of the upright will be blessed. Wealth and riches will be in his house, and his righteousness endures forever.

Colossians 1:15-20 NKJV He is the image of the invisible God, the firstborn over all creation. For by Him all things were created that are in heaven and that are on earth, visible and invisible, whether thrones or dominions or principalities or powers. All things were created through Him and for Him. And He is before all things, and in Him all things consist. And He is the head of the body, the church, who is the beginning, the firstborn from the dead, that in all things He may have the preeminence. For it pleased the Father that in Him all the fullness should dwell, and by Him to reconcile all things to Himself, by

Him, whether things on earth or things in heaven, having made peace through the blood of His cross.

Proverbs 22:4 NKJV By humility and the fear of the LORD are riches and honor and life.

Colossians 1 states how all things, whether things on earth or things in heaven, are being reconciled to Himself. I can't solidly claim money belongs to God, because it is a system of the world. God doesn't need money to support His kingdom, nor does He own money in Heaven to do this. However, we do!

Money's an important tool to surrender to God's use and will be for the building of His kingdom on earth. We, His temples are on earth. We must use money to live everyday while we are here. Unfortunately, this is the way or system that the world works through, we must have money to survive, and God desires that we survive excellently.

When we keep our hearts clear as we use and distribute money though His lead, God will help us prosper and have our own wealth. This is what I believe Deuteronomy 8:18 is speaking of. Verse 18 says, "And you shall remember the Lord Your God, for it is He who gives you power to get wealth, that He may establish His covenant which He swore to your fathers, as it is this day."

God doesn't mail us checks in the mail on a standard basis, but He does give us ideas, answers to hard situations, and always a way where there was no way in our finances. New inventive ideas are powerful, wise minds to build what is best is powerful and leads to wealth, which is from God.

As long as we are in the kingdom of God, here on earth, He wants to prosper us with the tools of the earth. As long as we are submitted to God's will, He will show us ways to use money in the very best ways. This is the way money is part of God's fruit in our lives, and tithing only accelerates His use and the main reason we should desire to tithe, is because God has flourished us on earth, and flourished through us, so then we tithe as a way of being grateful to Him.

Typically, when a friend or stranger has done something for me, I am very thankful, I try to give back out of my thankful heart. This is no different for our family's reason for tithing. No, you don't have to tithe to your church, but if you are grateful for it, and how it serves you, wouldn't you naturally want to give back somehow? Tithing is the perfect way to do that.

PRAYER

Father, open our eyes to the many new ways to use money for Your glory and not only for our gain alone. Keep our hearts pure of greed or gluttony with money and tithing to Your church. Starting today, I ask you to show me how my own use of money can glorify You Lord. Amen.

PROSPERITY

Day 24

How Jesus Used Money

Reading References

Luke 18:22-24 NKJV So when Jesus heard these things, He said to him, "You still lack one thing. Sell all that you have and distribute to the poor, and you will have treasure in heaven; and come, follow Me." But when he heard this, he became very sorrowful, for he was very rich.

And when Jesus saw that he became very sorrowful, He said, "How hard it is for those who have riches to enter the kingdom of God! For it is easier for a camel to go through the eye of a needle than for a rich man to enter the kingdom of God."

Luke 19:12-26 NKJV Therefore He said: "A certain nobleman went into a far country to receive for himself a kingdom and to return. So he called ten of his servants, delivered to them ten minas, and said to them, 'Do business till I come.' But his citizens hated him, and sent a delegation after him, saying, 'We will

not have this man to reign over us.' "And so it was
that when he returned, having received the kingdom,
he then commanded these servants, to whom he had
given the money, to be called to him, that he might
know how much every man had gained by trading.
Then came the first, saying, 'Master, your mina has
earned ten minas.' And he said to him, 'Well done,
good servant; because you were faithful in a very little,
have authority over ten cities.' And the second came,
saying, 'Master, your mina has earned five minas.'
Likewise, he said to him, 'You also be over five cities.'

"Then another came, saying, 'Master, here is your
mina, which I have kept put away in a handkerchief.
For I feared you because you are an austere man. You
collect what you did not deposit and reap what you
did not sow.' And he said to him, 'Out of your own
mouth I will judge you, you wicked servant. You
knew that I was an austere man, collecting what I did
not deposit and reaping what I did not sow. Why then
did you not put my money in the bank, that at my
coming I might have collected it with interest?'

"And he said to those who stood by, 'Take the mina
from him, and give it to him who has ten minas.' (But
they said to him, 'Master, he has ten minas.') 'For I
say to you, that to everyone who has will be given;
and from him who does not have, even what he has
will be taken away from him.

Matthew 17:24-27 NKJV When they had come to
Capernaum, those who received the temple tax came

to Peter and said, "Does your Teacher not pay the temple tax?"

He said, "Yes." And when he had come into the house, Jesus anticipated him, saying, "What do you think, Simon? From whom do the kings of the earth take customs or taxes, from their sons or from strangers?"

Peter said to Him, "From strangers."

Jesus said to him, "Then the sons are free. Nevertheless, lest we offend them, go to the sea, cast in a hook, and take the fish that comes up first. And when you have opened its mouth, you will find a piece of money; take that and give it to them for Me and you."

Jesus did not focus His ministry on money, but he did have to teach on money quite often and He needed money for ministry as well, as the Bible says, His ministry gave to the poor. He taught on money all throughout his ministry because people were greedy and unbalanced with its use all around Him. One thing that angered Him was the buying and selling at the temple, He took care of that, and I feel like it's a lesson in its own for us today about doing personal business at church. You can take that however you want but I choose not to risk it because of His response to the event, He was angry.

Jesus knew this unbalanced mindset would hinder the true understanding of prosperity and living in the kingdom which He was here to present. He knew some would get addicted to money, and others would steal it. But just as bad as that is, there would be some Christians who would call it heresy to have money, or prosperity (anything extra is prosperity) and then speak about how Christians should actually be poor, because it looked religiously humble, yet it is actually pious. Jesus corrected this type of mindset, and all those issues in His various teachings and conversations regarding money. Just read the Bible, it's all in there.

Money issues are a direct result of a larger heart issue, one that could really get new and elder Christians off the true track of the gospel message. Like in Matthew 17, when Jesus told Peter to go get a piece of money out of a fish's mouth to pay the temple tax as not to offend those who don't understand the Kingdom Jesus was presenting. It was a great lesson for Peter and yet it still applies today, and God provided for that situation as well.

Remember, God blesses us, money does not. If the mindset leans more towards worry about money needs, know this is a thinking Jesus redeemed each Christian from on the cross.

All our blessings in life naturally flow to the one who seeks the kingdom of God first. Seeking desperately for money is not a kingdom mindset. In the story of the talents in Luke 19, two of the servants understood the heart of the nobleman and diligently turned what was provided to them into more, but one did not understand and out of fear hid the one talent he was provided. This shows us we can go two ways when God blesses us with money. We can use it

108

wisely and gain more, or we can squander it or be selfish and have that taken away. This is an important lesson for us to remember and to teach our children about finances.

Whatever your financial situation is, God has an answer. Find scriptures for your personal situation and need, because honestly if you have a need in your life, it only means you haven't found the truth in the Word for that need just yet. Christians have been presented by Jesus Himself, into a life with no need. It tells me that in Psalm 23:1, The Lord is my Shephard; I shall not want.

The world has ever changing money need and concerns but not the kingdom. Our help comes from the Lord- through those who will be led by Him here on earth. Psalm 121:2 My help comes from the Lord, who made heaven and earth.

Seek out what the Bible says about money this week and whenever the enemy tries to throw a curveball where money is concerned you will be fully prepared and ready to hold your position of blessing without giving into worry.

PROSPERITY

PRAYER

Father, show me in Your Word Your money lessons I need to understand. Help me to uproot any untruth about money, and abundance for my life. Help me plant the truth of this understanding in the soil of my heart so they will grow the fruit of abundance and blessing all over my life. Show me then, where to bless, and who to bless and share this abundance within Your name, using my hands as Your own hands on the earth. I ask this of You, Father, in the name of Jesus. Amen.

CHAPTER 6

OUR FRUIT OF POSSESSIONS

PROSPERITY

Day 25

Possessions Are Also For the Kingdom's Use

Reading Reference

Matthew 6:19-21 NKJV "Do not lay up for yourselves treasures on earth, where moth and rust destroy and where thieves break in and steal; 20 but lay up for yourselves treasures in heaven, where neither moth nor rust destroys and where thieves do not break in and steal. 21 For where your treasure is, there your heart will be also.

Luke 18:22 NKJV So when Jesus heard these things, He said to him, "You still lack one thing. Sell all that you have and distribute to the poor, and you will have treasure in heaven; and come, follow Me."

Matthew seems the most explicit in stating the earthly treasures are less important than heavenly treasures. Why is earthly treasure less important? First, notice Matthew wasn't saying they are not important at all, just that they are less important than heavenly treasures. So earthly treasures could be money, literal gold and silver, or success, or having lots of beautiful things sitting around your house and in your driveway. Heavenly treasures are usually considered, the people we lead to Christ, the money we give to help serve the poor or needy to get by on. It can be our personal calls, and it is also of course the results of the gospel being preached. Earthly treasures are less important simply because they are not eternal. Where the heavenly treasures mentioned are eternal and will be brought back up to God, almost as an offering to Him.

Jesus goes even further in Luke 18 saying to sell all your earthly goods and use the money in areas of compassion for this is the way to gather treasure in heaven. The different areas of compassion are a various as there are people on earth, but they effect the person in a way that can win them, or prove to them there is a God, and He is a God who loves them enough to provide to them through that compassion.

It's more than just getting rid of our stuff, especially those things that may trip-up our Christian walk. If some 'thing' begins to draw you away from God, or keeps you distracted from your call, you are very dangerously close to that thing being an idol in your life. It's more about keeping my heart clear of idols. Idols would keep us stuck to them, and not selling those things we love can show we love them, more than Him. So many times, we may not even realize this is happening in our lives. Idols are sneaky and subtle; they certainly won't be obvious in the beginning of your relationship with them.

This is the main point of today's verses. Keeping a clear route to God without hinderances of idols.

114

Using possessions for the kingdom is very necessary too. It helps to forward the work of the gospel with out some ministry dealing with lack or working without using the best product. The kingdom of God deserves our best gifts, the best tools, and best purchases. This is also one way we can seek Him first, and the Kingdom.

PRAYER

Father, I thank you for helping me keep a clear route to You. Assist me in detecting when a possession is getting too possessive. Help me to see early on when something is not healthy in my life, and then also help me take the steps necessary to remove it. Keep my heart full of compassion and the desire to give to my fellow brother or sister if I can fulfill a need for them. Help me to get the things I am to share, so that I will have them on hand when that time arises for my brother. I ask you to keep my eyes open for each opportunity to share my possessions with whom you have in mind. Thank you for all you allow me to enjoy and possess. I ask all these things in the precious name of Jesus, Amen.

PROSPERITY

Day 26

Good Possessions Are From God

Reading Reference

2 Chronicles 32:29 NKJV Moreover he provided cities for himself, and possessions of flocks and herds in abundance; for God had given him very much property.

Proverbs 21: 5-6 NKJV The plans of the diligent lead surely to plenty, but those of everyone who is hasty, surely to poverty. Getting treasures by a lying tongue is the fleeting fantasy of those who seek death.

Ephesians 2:8 NKJV for by grace you have been saved thorough faith, and that not of yourselves; it is the gift of God,

1 Corinthians 7:7 NKJV For I wish that all men were even as I myself. But each one has his own gift from God, one in this manner and another in that.

God is the giver of the best gifts.

Take Hezekiah as an example in 2 Chronicles 32, where this king was honored obviously by the treasures God provided to Hezekiah.

117

PROSPERITY

The verses in Proverbs 21 compare how being diligent alone provides treasures plenty, but where a lying tongue actually can bring death. Consistency pays off eventually and the word says being diligent will also.

God gives great gifts; it is just that simple. Any believer whose heart is pure, and they seek the Lord God, as well as to please Him, are known to be rewarded for the place they give God in their life. God will lay this on the listening ear of other believers to do good to one another with gifts.

Some of the best gifts I have received were only thought in my heart that only God knew about. They came from quiet conversations with Him during our sporadic conversations daily. I talk to God a lot during the day, so He also has the capacity to speak back to me, directing and leading my day. Many times, this leading has brought me gifts from Him, happening just because He loves me. This is what made those gifts extra special.

Here is a second way to receiving these good gifts from God, we must ask. This is tough for some believers as it may look prideful to ask God for some grand possession. However, we are not to operate in pride ever, so Matthew 7 explains how we are to ask for not only the things we need, as God knows of the basic needs of His children, just like so many observant parents of children. God desires to operate the way it describes in Matthew 7, and I believe He enjoys giving us the things we ask for. Always remember to ask, even if you can do it by your own means.

Another thought is that in some of my life experiences I have come to understand the other view of this scripture. It doesn't say God give us everything we ever ask Him for. No! He is much wiser than that. He won't provide us possessions that will harm us or pull us from His foundational boundaries for our lives. He loves us too much to give us every little thing we have asked for. He absolutely will give us the good things. Those things will certainly bless our lives and flourish our relationship with Him. I am thankful God did not give me everything for which I have prayed.

PRAYER

Thank you, Father, for the many wonderful gifts You have placed into my life. Keep my heart clear to know if I am to give any of these gifts to a brother or sister and not keep them under my own roof. Keep me free from any fear of lacking in the giving You ask me to provide. Make me a blessing to other in the way You have blessed me so wonderfully. I desire to reflect this character trait of you to my fellow brethren of the faith. I ask these things in Jesus' name. Amen.

PROSPERITY

Day 27

We Have Possessions for Giving

Reading Reference

Matthew 2:11 NKJV And when they had come into the house, they saw the young Child with Mary His mother, and fell down and worshiped Him. And when they have opened their treasures, they presented gifts to Him: gold, frankincense, and myrrh.

In the same way these wise men in the Christmas story of Jesus' birth, sought Jesus knowing He was the Messiah, the Promised One, they honored Him with gifts specific for His future and wellbeing. We also must seek our Lord and give to Him from our abundance. We give to him, by giving to actual people around us, by giving to others, we give to God.

These gifts may not look like gold or precious oils, but they should surely be the best of our storehouses. More important than the physical gift given was the thankfulness and honor presented with the gifts. Gifts given out of a heart of love and honor offer to others true gifts with wrapping paper making them just as precious as the gift itself.

PROSPERITY

Thoughtful gifts are most desirable, so that would be different for each person to give to. The greatest gift we can give to God, who has anything and everything that is, would be our lives through salvation, and living a lifestyle which honors Him. This is the beautiful thing about the tradition of gift giving at Christmas and birthdays as a reminder and response to the greatest and best gift ever given from Him, being Jesus Christ.

PRAYER

Father, share with us your idea of gift giving so we can honor You well. Place in our hearts ideas for gifts we can give to others. Help us to always give from a heart of compassion and to listen to Holy Spirit for specific and perfect details in choosing gifts. Help us to also get better at giving gifts to those we don't know yet hear about their need. Help us to move quickly and firmly in our giving, being always ready and willing to give when an opportunity arises. Thank you, Father, for all that You give to us. Amen.

Day 28

Treasures Are Not Always Physical

Reading Reference

Matthew 12:35 NKJV A good man out of the good treasure of his heart brings forth good things, and an evil man out of the evil treasure brings forth evil things.

Colossians 2: 1-3 NKJV For I want you to know what a great conflict I have for you and those in Laodicea, and for as many as have not seen my face in the flesh, that their hearts may be encouraged, being knit together in love, and attaining to all riches of the full assurance of understanding, to the knowledge of the mystery of God, both of the Father and of Christ, in whom are hidden all the treasures of wisdom and knowledge.

2 Corinthians 4:7 NKJV But we have this treasure in earthen vessels, that the excellence of the power may be of God and not of us.

Matthew 12 says "a good man out of the good treasure of his heart…" by this we can know and understand the better gifts are not always physical.

PROSPERITY

Things from our heart, from our spirit-man and how God gives us understanding and knowledge not from man, can be the best gifts out of a heart of compassion.

2 Corinthians reminds us it isn't us who contains these treasures alone, but this power comes from God. He places those things in us and when we cultivate those gifts from God to maturity, they will naturally flow from us to be a blessing for others.

Beware though, as it also states there are other things that can be placed in our heart, not by God, but by the enemy, or from careless and hurting people, and if we feed on those things, they can also grow an evil painful fruit which would then contagiously flow from our own heart to others, moving as a cycle.

What are some of these good treasures? What do they look like?

Colossians 2 shows valuable things in life on earth, , wisdom and knowledge. This is not speaking of common or human knowledge. Today common knowledge is vast and at the touch of a smart phone or keyboard. This is what is known as the knowledge of man, and some of it is good, but none of it is perfect as God's knowledge is, which brings wisdom. In regard to natural knowledge, we can access at any time, which doesn't supply us wisdom. Wisdom is what we do with the knowledge we receive. Wisdom is the ability to decern and understand the knowledge we find. Wisdom and knowledge work hand in hand in the heart of the right people. Wisdom and knowledge also work hand in hand unto our perfection in Christ when we apply it. This wisdom and knowledge is the foundation for business ideas, answers to long held questions in life, and our creative ability to produce and construct items that didn't exist before it was birth in our spirit man. This is how God doesn't necessarily place money or wealth in our hands physically, but He does give the power (thoughts, and creative inventions) to obtain wealth and prosperity.

Deuteronomy 8:18 And you shall remember the Lord your God, for it is He who gives you power to get wealth, that He may establish His covenant which He swore to your fathers, as it is this day.

The richest treasures God gives will never be something we can initially touch physically.

PRAYER

Thank you, Father, for inventive ideas, perfect plans, and answers with wisdom to the questions we have little answers for in life. Help me daily to weed out the seeds of discord and hurt that could be placed into my heart's soil. Help me keep a pure motivation for wealth in the kingdom. I pray for increase as my goal for giving comes from increases above personal wealth. May I not measure wealth as the world measures wealth, but that I will keep a higher view of what the precious things are in life and focus on those. I ask this in the name of Jesus, amen.

PROSPERITY

Day 29

Don't Idolize Possessions

Reading Reference

Mark 10:22 NKJV Now as He was going out on the road, one came running, knelt before Him, and asked Him, "Good Teacher, what shall I do that I may inherit eternal life?" So Jesus said to him, "Why do you call Me good? No one is good but One, that is, God. You know the commandments: 'Do not commit adultery, "Do not murder,' 'Do not steal,' 'Do not bear false witness,' 'Do not defraud,' 'Honor your father and your mother.' " And he answered and said to Him, "Teacher, all these things I have kept from my youth."

Then Jesus, looking at him, loved him, and said to him, "One thing you lack: Go your way, sell whatever you have and give to the poor, and you will have treasure in heaven; and come, take up the cross, and follow Me."

But he was sad at this word, and went away sorrowful, for he had great possessions.

PROSPERITY

James 5:1-6 NKJV Come now, you rich, weep and howl for your miseries that are coming upon you! Your riches are corrupted, and your garments are moth-eaten. Your gold and silver are corroded, and their corrosion will be a witness against you and will eat your flesh like fire. You have heaped up treasure in the last days. Indeed the wages of the laborers who mowed your fields, which you kept back by fraud, cry out; and the cries of the reapers have reached the ears of the Lord of Sabaoth. You have lived on the earth in pleasure and luxury; you have fattened your hearts as in a day of slaughter. You have condemned; you have murdered the just; he does not resist you.

The alter sanctifies the sacrifice—Derick Prince [4]

We must be willing to sacrifice any possession we have obtained, no matter what the cost of that object.

The story of the rich young ruler in Mark 10 is an example of what making our possessions an idol can keep us from obtaining. He could have received so much more than his simple earthly possessions were worth, yet his heart was fixed on them. This thinking can keep us from obtaining what is truly rich, truly prosperous. The ruler's grand possessions were not his problem though by any means on their own. His heart position about these things he owned was the issue Jesus was pointing out to him. Jesus didn't need his money, or the sales his possessions produced, the one thing he lacked was his willingness to sell them and submit to Jesus. Maybe for you or me it isn't necessarily physical priceless possessions we have gained from the world, but it can be anything we place between ourselves and God, even offenses. Jesus wanted the ruler to see that his idolatry of the things he owned was the one thing he lacked giving up.

The rich ruler asked, "What shall I do that I may inherit eternal life?" Jesus' answer was removing the idols in your life ~ your 14-bedroom mansion, your Roles Roice, your rolling hills that produce the best wine in the land, and take up nothing but the gospel I give, receive it in return, and follow me around spreading this gospel. Follow what I do, and you will find eternal life— was the answer of Jesus, in my own paraphrased way.

What attachments do we need to let go of to have the answer from Jesus in our own story? Are we going to look at the world for satisfaction, or to the Christ for our eternal life and life on earth's satisfaction? Can we exchange the gain we see for the eternal satisfaction we cannot see with the eyes we use naturally?

Did you notice part of their conversation was about the commandments in the law, as Jesus verbally listed all the 'doing' commandments to him, but it was the most important, the 'being' commandment of have no other gods before Me which the rich ruler lacked.

Idolatry is sneaky and it's a constant issue to be filtered from our lives because this one comes like a thief in the night, undetected and in disguise most times.

PROSPERITY

It will be the compassion of Jesus and Holy Spirit; or maybe even a friend or church leader to point it out. However, if you come about being exposed to an idol in your life, steer clear of offense toward the one bringing it to your attention, because it's compassion for you that was noted firstly.

Think of this too, say you give a beautiful, exciting gift to your child or spouse one day for a birthday or Christmas gift. Then about two weeks later you want to spend time with that person, but they no longer want to spend time with you because that gift you gave is just too entertaining and consumes their time now. Wouldn't this item then have come between the two of you and before your established relationship? It projects rejection of the relationship and places the relationship and you as much less important to them than the gift.

The giver is now forced to be separated from the receiver and can no longer be an influencer or an important part of the life of the receiver, because the gift has now replaced the giver with priorities. I know I would be very hurt to be the giver in this senecio. I may even wish I had never given them the gift.

Personally, I don't ever want to do that to God. I know I have at some point in life about something. I am not advising in this lesson from anything outside of personal experience too. I am so grateful to the person who notices and is brave enough to call it out in any possible areas of idolatry they may notice. Why? Because that is love. That is them having true compassion for me and my walk with Jesus. My goal is to only worship God, and Him alone. I welcome interjection and accusation of this kind.

PRAYER

Father, may we realize quickly any true areas of idolatry from the good possessions in our lives. May we always surrender them if required to at any moment. Keep our hearts searching and pulling up the weeds of idolatry that begin to grow in our hearts. And may we listen to others' who call it out, when we have ignored Your own voice of warning and correction towards us first. I ask this in the precious name of Jesus. Amen.

CHAPTER 7

OUR FRUIT OF GOD'S FAITHFULNESS

Day 30
God's Faithfulness

Reading Reference

Isaiah 11:5 NKJV Righteousness shall be the belt of His loins, and faithfulness the belt of His waist.

1 Corinthians 1:9 NKJV God is faithful, by whom you were called into the fellowship of His Son, Jesus Christ our Lord.

Psalms 36:5 Your mercy, O Lord, is in the heavens; Your faithfulness reaches to the clouds.

Deuteronomy 7:9 NKJV Therefore know that the Lord your God, He is God, the faithful God who keeps covenant and mercy for a thousand generations with those who love Him and keep His commandments.

Lamentations 3:22-23 NKJV Through the Lord's mercies we are not consumed, because His compassions fail not. They are new every morning; great is Your faithfulness.

PROSPERITY

We have all heard the statement, 'God is faithful' but have we thought how deep His faithfulness goes? I included God's faithfulness in the prosperity series because consistency or faithfulness, produces a wealthy, prosperous life.

Lamentations 3 shows the consistency of God's faithfulness as being new every morning. The moment we wake each new morning His faithfulness is fresh. Once we became Christians, we have the opportunity to experience the bountiful faithfulness of God every day.

God's mercy is faithful. God's love is faithful. Most of all, God is faithful to the promises of His word. God being faithful is a fruit of prosperity in our lives. I sure hope you experience in your day to day walk just how faithful God is.

Most of the time these promises don't just show up in our laps each morning as we eat breakfast. His promises are readily available, but we must seek Him first, seek His ways, His heart and it is only then we truly experience the full abundance of what His faithfulness is, how it feels and works in our lives. I hope you make it a practice to seek Him first in all the things you endeavor to do. He doesn't intrude to be a part of the things that happen in our lives unless we ask Him to be a part. If you desire to experience God's faithful nature, just ask Him to show the many ways He has been in the past and then give Him opportunities to be that faithful Father He is famous for being.

134

Our Fruit of Christianity

I could write a whole book praising God for His faithfulness. He was faithful to me when He didn't have to be, and when I didn't deserve it. He was so real and faithful to his word in my life during some of the most traumatic days I lived out, and each quiet day full of peace just the same.

PRAYER

Father, thank you for your faithful ways. Thank you for our experience of knowing your faithfulness daily we understand how to carry out that faithfulness in our own lives to others. Today, I pray I will see clearly how to execute faithfulness in our work life and family life. This way Jesus' love can be seen through us. Thank you, Jesus, for establishing this request. Amen.

PROSPERITY

Day 31

Being Faithful to God

Reading Reference

Revelation 2:10 NKJV Do not fear any of those things which you are about to suffer. Indeed, the devil is about to throw some of you into prison, that you may be tested, and you will have tribulation ten days. Be faithful until death, and I will give you the crown of life.

1 Thessalonians 5:24 NKJV He who calls you is faithful, who also will do it.

Midmornings, on most days, I catch a glimpse of what's happening all around the world via news reports. I keep an eye on American news, but I keep a continuous gaze on what is happening in Isreal and its surrounding neighbors. So many days recently it has been one tragic story after another and that alone makes it harder to watch much news in one sitting.

This brings me back to how important it is for Christians today to be faithful in all God has asked us to do. Each of us have an assignment, each of us should be working in that assignment now. We are the literal hands and feet of the Gospel of Jesus, and this is important to Him that everyone knows about the option of life in Christ. Never think your part is too small, being faithful in the small things builds us for partaking in the big things so many times. One way we can have the nature of God is just by simply being faithful to what we know we are called to do.

The news headlines make our faithfulness vital to those around us. This is especially true for those who are working towards accomplishing our call while we have the time. It is obvious time is running short. Seeing all the news should never draw us back, out of fear, but know these things must happen, and push us with more fervor and diligence to being faithful in getting our own work accomplished in time. Doing my part of the work God relies on me to accomplish involves the skill and joy that comes with being faithful, no matter what I hear in the news.

Each of us have something clear and specific we are called to do for the kingdom of God. Building each other up in the holy faithfulness, and encouragement, even promoting one another are ways we can offer as being faithful with His work. Thereby our gifts only add sure foundations to support the whole body, every believer in his or her place, the whole church, in creating the thriving and prosperous purpose He built her for. I love the Body of Christ, each and every one in it, and I desire to see the whole-Body flourish as we bring the church age to its end.

Today, keep your minds on Him. Be faithful in His work and lay joy everywhere you go. Be the faithful light the world desperately needs. Bring peace to situations in chaos by being available at all times. Be the salt. Make kingdom news the headlines!

PRAYER

Father, help me see how important my faithfulness is to the success of your plan. Show me ways to bless those in the household of faith by my own consistent pursuit of spreading your kingdom and establishing all You placed me here to accomplish. I ask this Faithful Father, in the name of Your Son, Jesus. Amen.

PROSPERITY

Day 32

Jesus, Our Example of Faithfulness

Reading Reference

1 Thessalonians 5:24 NKJV He who calls you is faithful, who also will do it.

Hebrews 2:17 NKJV Therefore, in all things He had to be made like His brethren, that He might be a merciful and faithful High Priest in things pertaining to God, to make propitiation for the sins of the people.

Hebrews 3:1-2 NKJV Therefore, holy brethren, partakers of the heavenly calling, consider the Apostle and High Priest of our confession, Christ Jesus, who was faithful to Him who appointed Him, as Moses also was faithful in all His house.

Hebrews 10:23 NKJV Let us hold fast the confession of our hope without wavering, for He who promised is faithful.

PROSPERITY

I John 1:9 NKJV If we confess our sins, He is faithful and just to forgive us our sins and to cleanse us from all unrighteousness.

I like to look at the Bible as a road map of sorts for the Christian. Keeping in mind it was written for the Believer in Christ, or Christian committed to living for Jesus and not for the unsaved. I see excellent guidelines for our daily walk and for making decisions. I am a big believer that Jesus is our example, He is our only measuring stick to compare what we do with someone else to find success. He is also then our example of how to be faithful to God.

Jesus was obedient and faithful to the call He knew was on His own life in coming to earth and dying for those who had even rejected His father. God was not a new concept when Jesus came to earth so there were those who cursed God and despised Him even then. Jesus came and made the sacrifice for us anyway, faithfully. Jesus was faithful to the call and ministry for His life on earth. I am not sure I can say I have been fully faithful to my call, or ministry, but I can continue to walk that out and leave the past mistakes in the past.

Jesus was faithful to God during his treacherous death on earth. He was faithful in His teaching to His own disciples. Jesus was faithful to the church in His day, the church He was building in His ministry. Jesus was also faithful in His words, and faithful to the Bible and it's laid out structure, way of life while on this earth.

Following Jesus and using His example of ministry is an excellent guide. He is an excellent example of faithfulness on earth, and I will follow His lead. What he accomplished, I believe we also can accomplish through our own call, simply because He did it. He did this as a man.

PRAYER

Father, I seek today the grace and mercy to promote a faithful lifestyle, as Jesus showed me I can from the Word. Help me to understand what faithfulness looks like and feels like from Your perspective. I pray to stay faithful to You and to my assignment You have deemed necessary for me while on earth. Make my hands faithful hands, and my eyes to be faithful in seeing what you need me to see. I ask you to make my ears faithful to hear Your voice well. Assist me today in keeping my tongue in faithful alignment with Your Word, and Your will in my comings and goings to accomplish the call. Thank you for showing me how faithfulness is a part of Your prosperity, and that I also have a share in it. I ask each of these things in the name of Jesus, Amen.

PROSPERITY

Day 33
Faithfulness in Action

Reading Reference

Luke 16:10-12 NKJV He who is faithful in what is least is faithful also in much; and he who is unjust in what is least is unjust also in much. Therefore, if you have not been faithful in the unrighteous mammon, who will commit to your trust the true riches? And if you have not been faithful in what is another man's, who will give you what is your own?

Hebrews 3:1-2 NKJV Therefore, holy brethren, partakers of the heavenly calling, consider the Apostle and High Priest of our confession, Christ Jesus, who was faithful to Him who appointed Him, as Moses also was faithful in all His house.

Romans 3:3 NKJV For what if some did not believe. Will their unbelief make the faithfulness of God without effect?

Completing the call on my life requires faithful action every day. Every morning is a new opportunity to provide fellow Christians my skills and talents towards enhancing their kingdom experience here on earth. I do not accomplish this alone, which is why Christians are called the body of Christ. Meaning every person plays their part, like I do, to use skills and talents towards enhancing the kingdom while still here on earth.

I so enjoy listening to teachers who uncover vital truths from God's word for producing and living the enriched life in God's kingdom. There are countless hours of faithful study behind those equipping messages. Time spent separated and quiet, staying away from the hustle of the world's noise and chaos. This is an example of faithfulness in action.

Being faithful in the seemingly, insignificant quiet moments of study take consistent dedication to a selfless life. It was the selfless life of Jesus that awarded me eternal prosperity and health. I believe as we build the kingdom here on earth, we are also building our spiritual treasures in Heaven.

It's always the little unnoticed things that build and enhance our walk with the Lord. It is typically the same quiet, faithful person who cleans the church between services. Or the unnoticed nursery worker who is in their station long before church starts, and long after it finishes who may miss the fun conversations with friends, after or before church services three Sundays out of four a month. This is another example of faithfulness in action.

Remember, concrete is formed using small, unnoticeable stones working together, bound to create strong footholds for people to stand upon. Think of the Church body as this concrete, and each of us are unnoticeable stones when isolated, but when working together we make a strong foundation. I ask myself, what is the pebble I can add today to the foundation of God's kingdom for future users? Have you ever considered your own pebble or call and how it impacts the whole kingdom running the way God intends? I challenge you today to focus on this, focus on what you now contribute to the kingdom, and then follow up with thinking of how you can increase this impact and further fill the foundation of concrete for a sure foundation in the future.

PRAYER

Father, guide me in not skipping the tiny things. Help me to see the value in each step of creative work you have planned. Help me to see nothing as insignificant as that is the true part involved. Help me to fill the cracks of Your precious design that maybe others have disregarded as passed away. Help me to excel in even the irrelevant things I must complete. I ask these things in the name of Jesus, Amen.

PROSPERITY

NOTES

1 – Steps of Faith. (2018, June 10). Understanding Psalm 23: What God Meant by Green   Pastures and Still Waters. *Medium.* Retrieved June 28, 2025,
          from https://www.steppesoffaith.com/apologetics/un derstanding-psalm-23-god-green-   pastures-still-waters

2 - Gatlin, Justin. "All the "Fear Nots" in the Bible." *LOGOS Community*, Logos Community, 16   Nov. 2014, community.logos.com/discussion/98416/all-the-fear-nots-in-the-bible.

3- Strong, J. (1990). 4053 pĕrissŏs. In *New Strong's Exhaustive Concordance of the Bible* (Vol. 2, p. 70). Abundance definition.

4 - Prince, Derek. "Daily Devotional: How to Find God's Plan For Your Life." *Day 5: The Altar Sanctifies the Offering*, 2025, www.derekprince.com/devotionals/c-r014-005?fbclid=IwY2xjawLHsiVleHRuA2FlbQIxMQBicmlkETFrZl RtY2o4QXJwSmdoVVBaAR7cjclKeQC23m8YIdTbRsa-fxGrT_u2o0UGG7p4hlG2q3ma6A7fi8UXy44zWQ_aem_C7A RrCd1bFL4ANLxD.   Accessed 24 June 2025.

5 - Nelson, Thomas. *New King James Version*. N.p.: Bible Gateway, 1982. Accessed June 28,   2025 https://www.biblegateway.com.Scripture taken from the New King James Version®.   Copyright © 1982 by Thomas Nelson. Used by permission. All rights reserved.

PROSPERITY

MEET THE AUTHOR

Tamra Ingram-Curry was born and continues to reside in the beautiful Ozark Mountains with her husband and family. Before making a U-turn in life into writing and editing, Tamra was a hairdresser for 20 years.

The new writing direction was sparked by her obtaining a Bachelor of Arts in ministry. Later she continued in that path by obtaining a Bachelor of Science in Professional and Technical Writing, with a focus in Psychology, from Missouri State University.

As a writer of creative nonfiction, poetry, and storytelling Tamra uses her photography to teach and encourage positive lifestyle habits after trauma response and into trauma recovery.

Tamra has published a book, titled *Renew*, featuring a bit of her photography, along with works of poetry, which is currently on Amazon. One of her poetry works is featured in the 2016 compilation by Eber and Weinsteins' book titled, *Beyond the Sea*.

Tamra is also a fabric artist with other interests in painting and crocheting. However, her passion is found in playing drums, and she is featured on a Music Album by the band Laus Perennis entitled, *That Place*, which can be found on iTunes or Spotify.

Previous Books in Print for this Series

 *FOUNDATIONS* is the first book from the Series of *Our Fruit of Christianity* can be found in most bookstores and several online options as well. Foundations is the first devotion book in the five-volume series of Our Fruit of Christianity Devotions. This series explores the many blessings and fruits we cultivate and share as Christians and servants of Christ. In Foundations, we cover foundational topics such as trust, standing, peace, worship, and prayer, among others.

Each devotion is accompanied by a separate study journal to enhance your study experience, making it ideal for personal reflection or as an excellent guide for group settings.

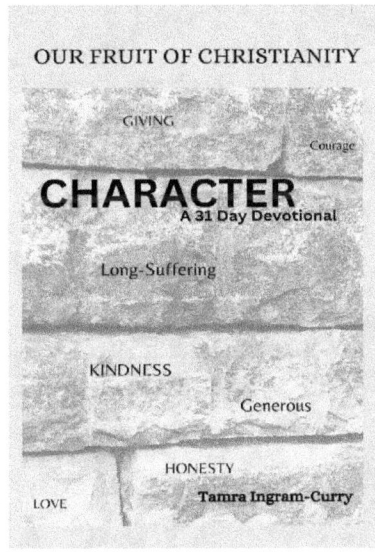

CHARACTER is the second book from the series *Our Fruit of Christianity* and can be found in most bookstores and several online purchasing options as well. Character is key to our everyday life. This second edition of **Our Fruit of Christianity Devotions** on Character is a detailed look at Christian character we can attain, like Christ exampled to us. In **Character**, topics of character such as kindness, courage, humility, suffering and love, are explored, among others.

Each devotional book in the series is accompanied by a separate study journal to enhance your study experience, making it ideal for a deep personal reflection, or as an excellent guide for group settings.

CURRY PUBLISHING

Our Fruit of Christianity

PROSPERITY

www.ingramcontent.com/pod-product-compliance
Lightning Source LLC
Chambersburg PA
CBHW071259130626
46556CB00003B/1386